The Mailbox® Monthly Idea Books— Your Ultimate Monthly Resource!

Your friends at *The Mailbox®* have taken monthly books to a whole new level! We've created a Web site that contains even more classroom resources to complement the hundreds of curriculum-based activities in each book. We've also added skill lines to each idea for a quick curriculum reference at a glance. Plus, every book has a comprehensive index to make planning and selecting activities even easier! All of these terrific features make this series of monthly books one that you can't be without!

Now Internet Interactive!

- For each book, you'll enjoy over **50 pages** of online resources such as patterns, recording sheets, reproducibles, and classroom forms!
- You'll find **new** resources for **every** thematic unit in each book!
- Many classroom forms can be **filled out online** and printed. No more handwritten versions!
- Web site content is tailored to you and your **grade level.**
- **All** reproducibles and pattern pages from each monthly book are available online for **easy printing.**
- Access is absolutely **FREE!**

Getting your online extras is as easy as 1, 2, 3!

1. Go to **www.themailboxbooks.com** and click on "Add a book."
2. Complete the simple registration form.
3. Follow the on-screen instructions to add your book.

Look for the computer icon 🖥 throughout each book to guide you to your FREE online extras.

About This Book

It's hard to believe we could improve on our best-selling series of monthly idea books—but we have! In this edition, you'll find the following exciting new features added to our irreplaceable collection of curriculum-based ideas!

- A Web site containing *even more* classroom resources complements the hundreds of activities provided in each book. (To access this incredible site for free, follow the simple instructions found on page 1.)
- A skill line for each idea provides a curriculum reference at a glance.
- A comprehensive index makes selecting and planning activities a breeze!

We think you'll agree that these new features make this series of monthly books the best ever!

Managing Editors: Scott Lyons, Deborah G. Swider
Editor at Large: Diane Badden
Contributing Writers: Darcy Brown, Rebecca Brudwick, Lisa Buchholz, Stacie Stone Davis, Amy Erickson, Heather E. Graley, Jill Hamilton, Cynthia Holcomb, Nicole Iacovazzi, Lisa Kelly, Brenda McGee, Sharon Murphy, Susan Hohbach Walker
Copy Editors: Lynn Bemer Coble, Gina Farago, Karen Brewer Grossman, Amy Kirtley-Hill, Karen L. Mayworth, Jennifer Rudisill, Debbie Shoffner
Cover Artist: Clevell Harris
Art Coordinator: Theresa Lewis Goode
Artists: Jennifer Tipton Bennett, Pam Crane, Theresa Lewis Goode, Nick Greenwood, Clevell Harris, Susan Hodnett, Ivy L. Koonce, Sheila Krill, Mary Lester, Rob Mayworth, Clint Moore, Greg D. Rieves, Kimberly Richard, Rebecca Saunders, Barry Slate, Donna K. Teal
Typesetters: Lynette Dickerson, Scott Lyons, Mark Rainey
Indexer: Laurel Robinson
The Mailbox® Books.com: Kimberley Bruck (manager); Debra Liverman, Sharon Murphy (associate editors); Jennifer L. Tipton (designer/artist); Troy Lawrence, Stuart Smith (production artists); Karen White (editorial assistant); Paul Fleetwood, Xiaoyun Wu (systems)

President, The Mailbox Book Company™: Joseph C. Bucci
Director of Book Planning and Development: Chris Poindexter
Book Development Managers: Cayce Guiliano, Elizabeth H. Lindsay, Thad McLaurin, Susan Walker
Curriculum Director: Karen P. Shelton
Traffic Manager: Lisa K. Pitts
Librarian: Dorothy C. McKinney
Editorial and Freelance Management: Karen A. Brudnak
Editorial Training: Irving P. Crump
Editorial Assistants: Terrie Head, Hope Rodgers, Jan E. Witcher

JUNE, JULY, & AUGUST

Table of Contents

Cooking Up
NEW FRIENDSHIPS

Serve up a batch of these fun-filled activities to help your students foster new friendships. Beware, students might just ask for seconds!

ideas by Stacie Stone Davis and Jill Hamilton

Recipes for Friendship 🖥
Identifying characteristics valued in friendship, descriptive writing

A pinch of humor, a dash of kindness, and a whole lot of understanding are the ingredients needed to ensure a lasting friendship! Enlist your students' help in naming characteristics (or ingredients) that help friendships flourish. List students' responses on the chalkboard. Afterward, give each child a construction paper recipe card like the one shown. Using the class-generated list for assistance, have each child write his own recipe for friendship. Then invite interested volunteers to share their recipes with classmates. Mount the recipe cards on a bulletin board that has been decorated with a large construction paper cooking pot. Spice up the bulletin board display by mounting students' photographs (or self-portraits) on the board too. Add the title "Recipes for Friendship" and you've got yourself a mighty fine bulletin board!

Recipe for ___friendship___

Ingredients:
1. kindness
2. a dash of humor
3. lots of understanding

Directions:
1. Talk nice.
2. Play with them at recess.
3. Work problems out.

RECIPES FOR FRIENDSHIP

Buddy Boxes
Following directions, responding to questions

Buddy Boxes will give your students the opportunity to start new friendships. Provide each child with a light construction paper copy of the box pattern on page 8. To make a Buddy Box, each student completes the questions on the box pattern as desired. Then, to assemble the box, she cuts along the heavy solid lines, folds on the dotted lines, and then tapes the squares together to form a box. (Provide assistance as needed.)

Once the boxes are complete, let the fun begin! Pair students. Instruct one partner to roll his box and read the question that lands faceup; then have the other partner answer the question. Have students repeat this process, as time permits, alternating the roles of roller and responder.

When did you get your bicycle?

What is your favorite ice cream?

Poetry Pals 🖥
Writing poetry

This cooperative poetry-writing activity is sure to result in some poems with panache. To begin, share some friendship-related poetry of your choice. Then invite students to create their own friendship poems. Pair students and supply each twosome with a poetry frame similar to the one shown. Have each student pair work together to complete and illustrate the poetry frame. Invite interested volunteers to share their poems with classmates. Then bind the poems between construction paper covers to create a classroom anthology titled "A Friend to the End."

A friend is someone who _____ and _____.
A friend never _____
or _____.
A friend is _____,
_____, and
_____.

I'm glad that you're my friend!

by_____ and _____
      student   student

We Go Together
Recognizing word pairs, playing cooperatively

Like bagels and cream cheese or peanut butter and jelly, good friends go together! Challenge your students to name other items that go together, such as a baseball and a bat or bread and butter. To do this, pair students and provide each pair with a sheet of writing paper. On a given signal, instruct each student pair to begin listing things that go together. Allow students to work for a predetermined time period. At the end of the brainstorming session, have each pair share its list with the class. List students' responses on the board.

Then, for a fun variation, use students' list ideas to make a Memory Game. To make the game, select a pair of words from the list. Print one of the words from the pair on an index card, and print the corresponding word on another index card. Repeat this process until you have at least 20 cards. To play, a student pair places all the cards facedown on a playing surface. In turn, each player turns over two cards. If the cards match—or go together—the player keeps the cards and turns over two more cards. If the cards do not match, the player turns them facedown again. Play continues in this manner until all the cards have been matched. The player with the most cards at the end of the game wins!

In a Jam 🖥
Recognizing that behaviors have consequences

Survey your students to determine if they've ever found themselves in a sticky situation with a friend. If your students are like most, chances are they have been, at one time or another, in a jam. Use this role-playing activity to help students develop strategies to deal with these uncomfortable situations. To prepare for this activity, cut several strawberry shapes from red construction paper. On each cutout write a situation similar to the ones shown. Store the cutouts in a jelly jar or another suitable container. To begin the activity, have one volunteer select a berry cutout and read the situation aloud. Invite students to describe solutions to the situation. After discussing the possible consequence of each solution, have the class decide which solution works best and why. Model this procedure several times; then divide students into a desired number of groups. Ask one member from each group to select a berry. Then have each group repeat the problem-solving process practiced earlier. For a fun and educational finale, invite each group to role-play its situation for the class.

You see someone picking on another kid...

You need help...

You want to join a game...

A Tutti-Frutti Friendship Party

Conclude your unit on friendship on an upbeat note: make placemats on which to serve bowls full of Friendship Salad that your students have helped to prepare.

Friendship Placemats
Demonstrating a weaving technique, recognizing positive traits in others

Students will empty their plates in a hurry in order to read these personalized placemats. To make a placemat, a student folds a 9" x 12" sheet of construction paper in half lengthwise. Then she uses a pencil and a ruler to draw parallel lines from the fold. The lines should be about 3 1/2" in length and spaced about two inches apart. Then, starting from the fold, she cuts on each of the resulting lines (taking care to leave a one inch border along the edge). Next, she unfolds the paper, and weaves three 2" x 12" construction paper strips through the resulting slits. She then glues the ends of each strip to the paper mat. To complete the projects, have students write positive comments about their peers on the placemats. To do this, have each student stand behind her desk with her placemat in hand.

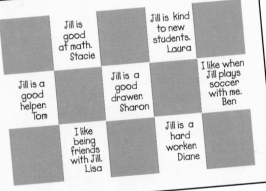

Next, begin playing a musical recording. While the music is playing, have each student circulate around the room. Then stop the music. When the music stops, each child locates the nearest student, trades placemats, and writes a positive comment about that student. Repeat this process as time permits. If desired, laminate the place-mats for durability. After all, these are placemats that children will want to read again and again!

Friendship Salad
Collecting data, creating a graph

This Friendship Salad is sure to be a hit with your youngsters! To make the salad, ask each student to bring to school a resealable bag filled with two cups of his favorite fruit. Ask that the fruit be prewashed and cut into bite-size pieces. Mix all of the fruit into a large bowl; then add two cups of orange juice. Afterward, place a bowl of the Friendship Salad atop each child's placemat. When students have had their fill of Friendship Salad, provide each child with a copy of the "Circle of Friends" reproducible on page 9. Challenge each student to survey her friends and record the findings on her sheet.

Clevell Harris

Books You Can Sink Your Teeth Into

Enjoy this helping of friendship-related books.

Yo! Yes? 🖥

written and illustrated by Chris Raschka
Organizing information on a diagram

This Caldecott honor book is a simple story about two strangers who meet on the street and become friends. After reading and discussing the story with your students, ask each student to complete a Friendship Diagram. To do this, have each student choose a partner. Provide each student pair with a diagram similar to the one shown. To complete the project, each student analyzes the traits he has in common with his partner and the traits he considers to be uniquely his.

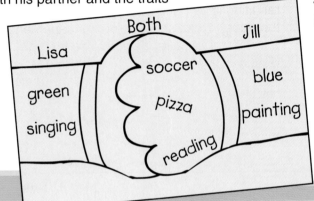

Lisa — green, singing
Both — soccer, pizza, reading
Jill — blue, painting

Friends

written and illustrated by Helme Heine
Making a personal connection

Charlie Rooster, Johnny Mouse, and fat Percy are good friends who always stick together. But when the friends try to plan a slumber party, obstacles get in their way. Finally, the friends conclude that sometimes friends can't be together—but they can dream about the next time they will be. After sharing the story, plan a class slumber party. Hold the slumber party during school hours and invite students to wear their pajamas and bring their sleeping bags. During the party, ask students to draw pictures of exciting adventures that they would like to take part in with their friends.

Wilfrid Gordon McDonald Partridge

written by Mem Fox
Developing intergenerational relationships

Wilfrid Gordon McDonald Partridge is a young boy who lives next door to a nursing home. He likes to visit there, and forms a special bond with Miss Nancy. Although Wilfrid isn't sure what a memory is, he does know that Miss Nancy is missing hers. But during his visits he learns that by sharing his memories with Miss Nancy, he helps her find some of hers.

After reading this story, tell students that friendships can be formed with people of any age. Explain to students that when you make a new friend it's like opening a door to a whole new world. Afterward, invite each student to interview an older friend. This person could be a neighbor, a family friend, or a relative. During the interview, encourage students to ask questions like the following: What was your favorite food when you were little? How did you celebrate the holidays? Remind students that they should share their memories too. Ask each child to bring a photograph of his elderly friend to school, if possible.

After the interview process is complete, have each student make one of these special keepsake projects. To make a project, each child turns a 6" x 9" piece of brown construction paper lengthwise, runs a trail of glue along the left edge, and glues the paper to a 9" x 12" sheet of colored construction paper as shown. Next, she decorates the brown paper to resemble a door and then prints "Meet [name of senior citizen]" above the door. Then she folds back the door and glues a photograph (or a crayon drawing) in the resulting space. Finally, she writes information about the featured person around the photograph. Mount the completed projects on a bulletin board titled "Opening the Door to New Friendships."

Meet Christine Stone

had 3 kids

...sed to ...ide a pig

Pattern
Use with "Buddy Boxes" on page 4.

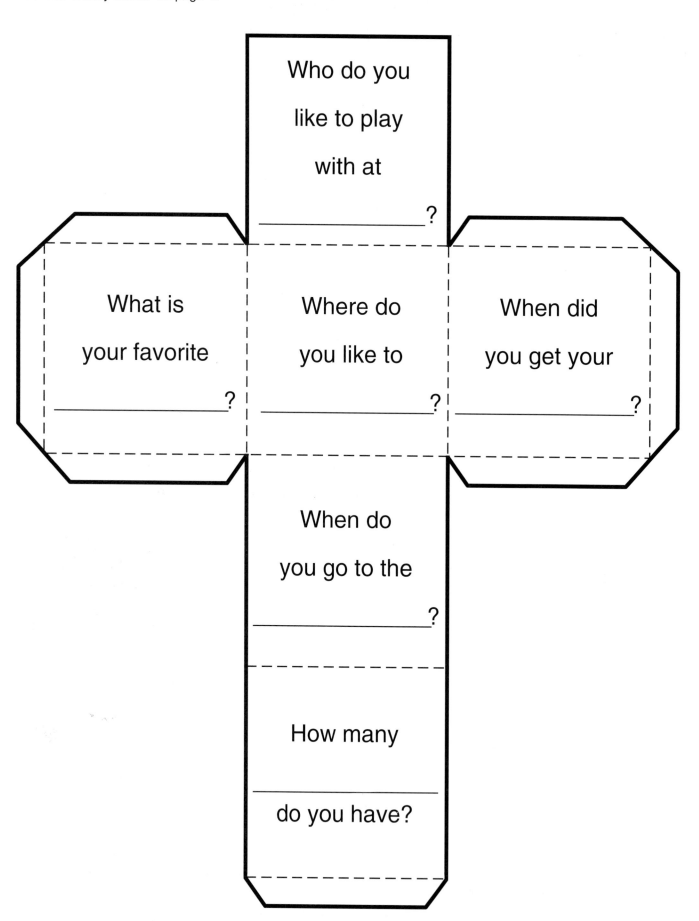

Who do you
like to play
with at
_____?

What is
your favorite
_____?

Where do
you like to
_____?

When did
you get your
_____?

When do
you go to the
_____?

How many
_____
do you have?

Name _____

Circle of Friends

Ask each of eight friends which fruit he or she likes best.
Use tally marks to count.

apple	strawberry	orange

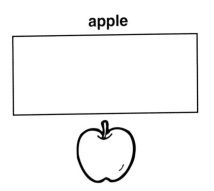  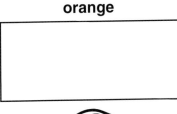

Count the results.

How many friends like apples the best? _____

How many friends like strawberries the best? _____

How many friends like oranges the best? _____

Use the information to make a pie graph.
Color one pie piece green for each friend who likes apples best.
Color one pie piece red for each friend who likes strawberries best.
Color one pie piece orange for each friend who likes oranges best.

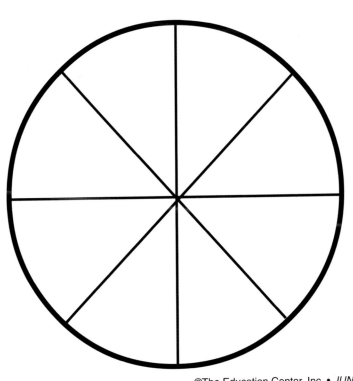

Analyze the results.

Which fruit was most popular?

_____

Which fruit was least popular?

_____

Note to the teacher: Use after "Friendship Salad" on page 6.

The Great Outdoors

Load up your backpack and lace up your hiking boots! This unique collection of learning activities will have your students feeling right at home with nature. Whether singing campfire songs or making bird feeders, your students are sure to have a memorable experience!

ideas by Darcy Brown and Rebecca Brudwick

"Tee-rific" T-Shirts!
Following directions

Set the stage for your class's experience in the great outdoors with these "tee-rific" T-shirts. In advance, cut several outdoor-related sponge shapes, such as trees, birds, tents, and stars. Also obtain a variety of fabric paints and colored permanent markers, and a classroom supply of discarded newspapers.

To begin, ask each student to bring to school a clean, white T-shirt. When the shirts have been brought in, have each youngster paint a camping T-shirt. To do this, she layers sheets of newspaper in between the front and back of her shirt. She then dips one side of a sponge cutout into a desired color of fabric paint and presses it firmly on her shirt. She removes the sponge and uses a new one to repeat the process with a different color of paint. When the paint is dry, she uses the permanent markers to add desired details to her shirt. Encourage your youngsters to wear their T-shirts as they participate in the following activities.

Mary Lester

Camping Memories
Descriptive writing

These nifty journals provide youngsters with a great way to keep up with their "camping" memories. To make a journal, a student cuts out a construction paper copy of the tent pattern on page 17. Next, she traces the tent pattern onto five sheets of writing paper; then she cuts out the resulting tent shapes and staples them behind the construction paper cover. To complete her journal, she adds the title "My Camping Journal" and desired decorations to the front cover. Set aside time for students to write in their journals every day. Encourage youngsters to describe their favorite camping activities. Your students will be eager to take their journals home to share with their families.

Badges of Safety
Defining safety strategies

Encourage safe student behaviors with this one-of-a-kind idea. Challenge your students to brainstorm safety rules concerning fires, wild animals, and common sense while camping or playing outside. List students' responses on the chalkboard. Then have each student use a copy of the badge pattern (page 19) to depict a safety rule. To do this, the youngster writes a safety rule on the provided lines and illustrates the rule as desired. Next, he cuts out his badge and glues it atop a slightly larger construction paper circle. Collect the badges and mount them on a bulletin board titled "Earn Your Safety Badge!" What a great way to promote student safety!

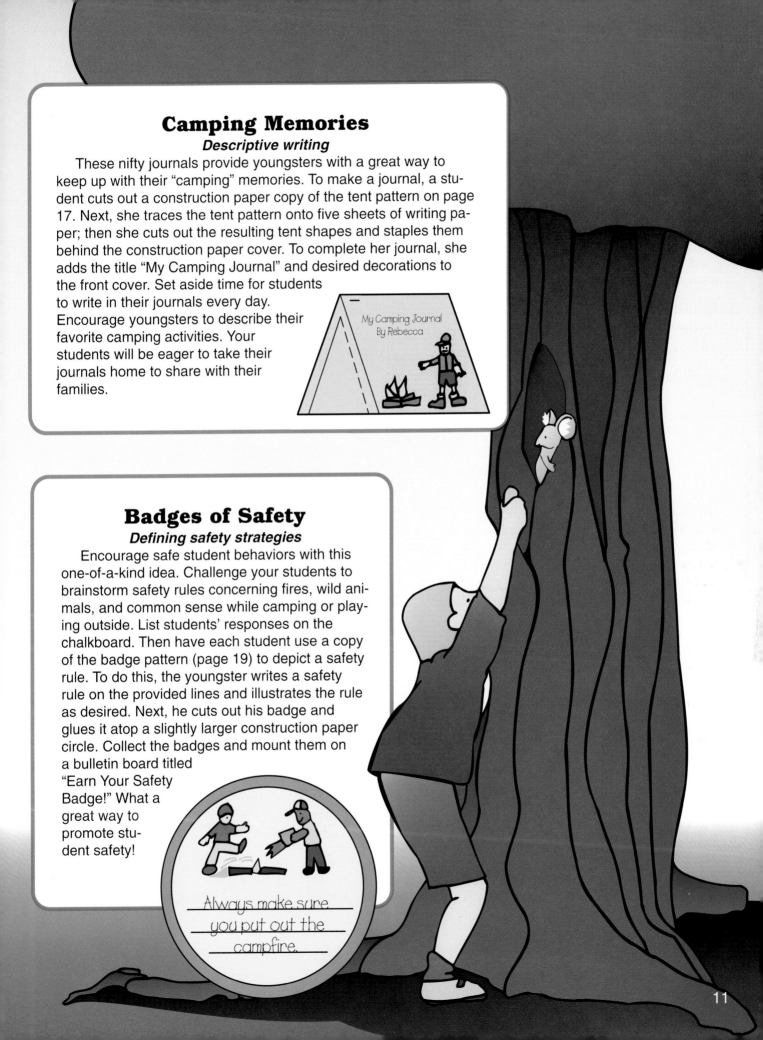

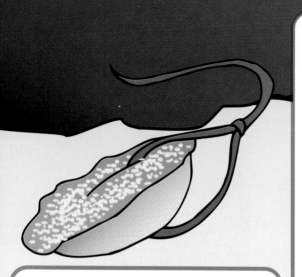

Birds of a Feather
Recording observations, drawing conclusions

Turn your youngsters on to bird-watching—a hobby that can last a lifetime! After students have made bird feeders (see "Bonny Bird Feeders"), invite them to observe the birds who frequent the feeders. Give one copy of the bird observation sheet (page 18) to each student. Instruct each student to observe one bird at the bird feeders for a predetermined amount of time. Challenge each student to complete his sheet while he's observing the bird. Back in the classroom, have each student use the information he gathered and bird-related reference materials to determine the type of bird he watched. After he has completed his sheet, have him cut it out, fold his paper in half, and then write his name and draw desired illustrations on the front cover. Then have him copy and complete the sentence starter "I have learned that this bird…" on the back cover. For an additional activity, invite a member from the local Audubon Society to speak to your students about birds. No doubt your budding ornithologists will take note of the wealth of information she's sure to provide!

Bonny Bird Feeders
Recognizing a basic need

Attract a bounty of birds with these easy-to-make bird feeders! Obtain one half of a plain bagel for each student. To make a feeder, the student spreads peanut butter on the cut side of a bagel and then presses the bagel into a shallow pan of birdseed. Next, she threads a length of yarn through the hole in the middle of the bagel and ties the yarn's ends. Suspend the completed feeders from trees around your school to attract a flock of fine-feathered friends.

Towering Trees
Using an art technique, working cooperatively

Bring the forest into your classroom with this "tree-mendous" art activity! Divide your students into groups of four. Give each student in a group one 9" x 12" sheet of white construction paper and several six-inch squares of white construction paper. Have students take their papers, crayons, and a book or clipboard outside to a predetermined area. If possible, assign a different tree to each group of students. Instruct the group members to make brown crayon rubbings of the tree trunk using the large sheets of construction paper; then have them create leaf rubbings on the small pieces of construction paper with their green crayons. (Be sure to tell students to place their books or clipboards behind the construction paper *before* making leaf rubbings.) Then challenge each group to identify its type of tree.

Back in the classroom, instruct each group to glue the four sheets of large construction paper together to create a tree trunk as shown. Then have students overlap the leaf rubbings at the top of the trunk and glue them together to create the leaves of the tree. If desired, have each group cut birds and nests from construction paper scraps and add them to its tree. When these projects are dry, mount them around the walls of your classroom for a fabulous forest effect!

"Tent-alizing" Teasers 🖥

Using manipulatives to solve word problems

Enhance your little campers' word problem skills with this math center. Make copies of the tent pattern (page 17) on construction paper. Laminate the tents for durability; then cut each tent along the dotted line. Use a wipe-off marker to program each tent with a different problem similar to the ones shown; then lift the flap and write the answer to the problem on the back. Place the tents and miniature marshmallows at a math center. A student selects a tent, uses the marshmallows to solve the problem, and then lifts the flap to check his work. Reprogram the tents throughout your unit to keep youngsters on their toes with solving word problems.

Sue and Alice counted 5 robins, 4 cardinals, 2 deer, and 1 blue jay. How many birds did Sue and Alice spot?

The campers have 12 hot dogs and 2 packages that each contain 8 buns. How many more buns than hot dogs do they have?

Jerry has 4 mosquito bites. Bob has 5 more bites than Jerry. Sue has 1 less bite than Bob. How many mosquito bites does Sue have?

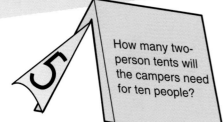

How many two-person tents will the campers need for ten people?

Sing It Loud! 🖥

Participating in rhyme and song

Teach your youngsters this fun camping song and its accompanying motions. Invite students to make up additional verses and hand actions to go with the song.

While on a Camping Trip!
(sung to the tune of "Here We Go Round the Mulberry Bush")

This is the way we pitch a tent, Pitch a tent, pitch a tent. This is the way we pitch a tent While on a camping trip.	*Extend arms above head, palms together and fingers pointing up.*
This is the way we build a fire, Build a fire, build a fire. This is the way we build a fire While on a camping trip.	*Pretend to lay logs on a fire.*
This is the way we look at birds, Look at birds, look at birds. This is the way we look at birds While on a camping trip.	*Curl fingers like binoculars and look through them.*

What's Abuzz?

Narrative writing

What's abuzz? Why, bees, of course! Invite your youngsters to share some bee experiences they have had while camping or on a picnic. Then challenge each youngster to write a story about his actual bee experience (or an imaginary one). First he writes his story on a 4" x 6" piece of writing paper; then he glues it to the center of a 6" x 8" piece of yellow construction paper. Next, he presses his thumb on a black stamp pad and then makes a thumbprint on the yellow construction paper border. He uses a black, fine-tipped permanent marker to add bee details—such as wings, antennae, and legs—to his thumbprint. He repeats the printing and drawing process, creating a bee border around his story. Collect the bee stories and mount them on a wall or bulletin board with the title "What's Abuzz?"

One day, I was playing outside with my sister. A bee buzzed by my head. He saw me and started to chase me. He chased me all the way home.

The End

Sammy

Celestial Sights

Understanding that stars form patterns in the sky

Invite your youngsters to re-create in your classroom a nighttime sky that's perfect for stargazing, a favorite camping activity. Have students browse through books or reference materials that contain pictures of constellations. Explain to students that the constellations were given their names by people who saw dot-to-dot outlines of things among the stars. Next, ask each student to select a constellation to re-create. Provide each youngster with a sheet of black construction paper and a small square of glow-in-the-dark paper (available at art supply stores). To create a constellation, the student hole-punches the square of glow-in-the-dark paper; then she glues the punches on the black paper in the shape of the desired constellation. When the glue is dry, she draws lines with chalk to connect the cutouts. Mount the constellations on or near the ceiling. Then turn off the lights and let the stargazing begin!

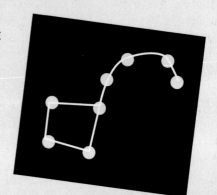

Bird Catcher

Engaging in physical activity, following directions

This outdoor game will have your youngsters flying with excitement! To begin, designate two goal lines approximately 25 yards apart. Name one goal "forest" and the other goal "bird nest." Select one youngster to be the Bird Catcher. Then assign different bird names (such as blue jay, robin, eagle, hawk, or crow) to the remaining students. Have the Bird Catcher stand in the area between the forest and the bird nest, and have the rest of the class stand in the forest. To play the game, the Bird Catcher calls out a bird's name. The students assigned that name flap their arms and pretend to "fly" to the bird nest as the Bird Catcher tries to catch them. If a child is caught (tagged), he is out and must stand to the side of the playing area. Then the Bird Catcher calls another name, and those students fly and the chase continues. After the Bird Catcher has called two or three bird names, he shouts, "All birds fly!" and the remainder of the students try to fly to the bird nest without being caught. At the end of the game, invite the Bird Catcher to select a *new* Bird Catcher from the birds who made it safely to the nest. Then reassign bird names and have students play the game again!

A-camping We Will Go!

Sharing personal opinions

Culminate your great outdoors unit with a classroom camp-out! Ask students to bring a sleeping bag or blanket to school on a designated day. Also invite them to wear their "tee-rific" T-shirts (see page 10). Have students place their sleeping bags in a circle on the floor. Then enlist the students' help in creating a simulated campfire. To do this, create a fire pit with a supply of rocks; then use paper-towel rolls and construction paper flames to build an imaginary fire. For a tasty treat, serve Camper's Delight or have your students make Supreme S'mores (see the recipes below). Then turn off the lights for a little "stargazing" and read a story aloud by flashlight (see "Literature for Nature Lovers!" on page 16 for suggested titles). To conclude the unit, ask each child to share his opinion of camping with the class. Then present each youngster with a personalized copy of the certificate on page 19.

Supreme S'mores

(Serves 1)

Each student needs the following:

1 whole graham cracker (split in half)
1 miniature candy bar
1 spoonful of marshmallow creme

Spread the marshmallow creme onto one graham cracker. Place the candy bar on top of the creme. Then top with the other graham cracker.

Camper's Delight

(Serves 15)

You'll need the following:

2 c. miniature marshmallows
2 c. milk chocolate chips
4 c. Golden Grahams® cereal
1/2 c. shelled sunflower seeds
2 c. raisins

Mix all the ingredients in a large bowl, and serve portions in small cups or resealable plastic bags.

Literature for Nature Lovers!

Three Days on a River in a Red Canoe
by Vera B. Williams
Recalling details, making a personal connection

When a young boy finds a red canoe for sale in a yard on his way home from school, the adventure has only just begun. After reading this story aloud, ask students to name some of the activities the boy's family participated in while on the canoe trip. List students' responses on the chalkboard. Then invite each youngster to copy and complete the sentence starter "If I had a red canoe, I would..." on a strip of writing paper. Next, have him glue his strip to a red canoe cutout. After students have shared their sentences with their classmates, collect the canoes and staple them to a bulletin board with the title "Red Canoe Adventures." What can you do in a red canoe? Plenty!

If I had a red canoe, I would take a trip to Ohio. I would go fishing there.

When Daddy Took Us Camping
by Julie Brillhart
Increasing auditory memory

In this story set to rhyme, a young family finds that exciting adventures await them in their own backyard. Ask your students to imagine that they are going on a camping trip and must remember all their supplies. Then invite your students to sit in a circle on the floor to play this campfire game. Select a student to start the game by reciting the following sentence: "Daddy is taking us camping, and I will bring a _____." Have him complete the sentence with an item that he would bring on a camping trip. Then have the child to his left recite the first student's sentence and then add an item of her own. Continue the game in the same manner, with each new student repeating the previously mentioned items and adding one of her own. This challenging game will have your little campers concentrating on fun!

Bailey Goes Camping
by Kevin Henkes
Responding to literature

Bailey can't wait to grow up! He wants to go camping with his older siblings, but he's too young. Like Bailey, many of your youngsters may have had similar experiences. Use this story to encourage students to discuss their feelings about these situations. After sharing the book, have youngsters sit in a circle on the floor and discuss how Bailey felt when he was left out of the camping trip. Then ask each student to think about a time he felt left out. Pass a flashlight around the circle as youngsters share their feelings. For an added challenge, pass the flashlight around a second time and have each student think of alternative activities in which he could have participated.

More Nature-Lover Literature!

Pitch a tent in the corner of your classroom and invite your youngsters to read the following stories while in it:

- *Amelia Bedelia Goes Camping* by Peggy Parish
- *Boat Ride With Lillian Two Blossom* by Patricia Polacco
- *Pinky and Rex and the Double-Dad Weekend* by James Howe
- *Rusty's Red Vacation* by Kelly Asbury
- *When I Go Camping With Grandma* by Marion Dane Bauer

Use the tent with "Camping Memories" on page 11 and " 'Tent-alizing' Teasers" on page 13.

Bird Observation Sheet

Use with "Birds of a Feather" on page 12.

Draw a picture of the bird.

The bird is a _____.

©The Education Center, Inc. • JUNE, JULY, & AUGUST • TEC759

On the Lookout for Birds!

Color

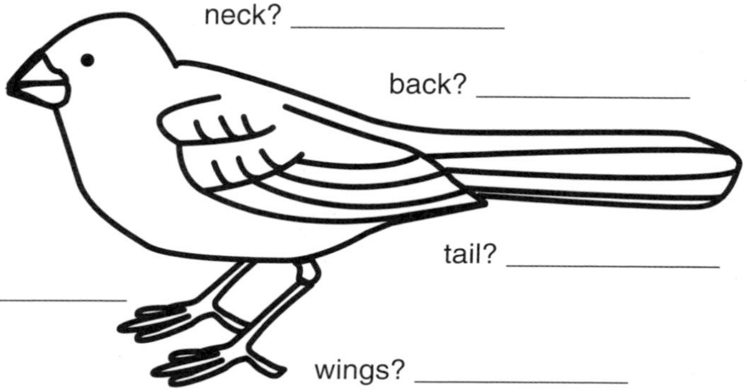

crown? _____

neck? _____

breast? _____

back? _____

tail? _____

wings? _____

Shape and Size
Check one for each.

body

____ slender

____ plump

legs

____ long

____ short

tail

____ pointed on end

____ square on end

beak

____ long

____ short

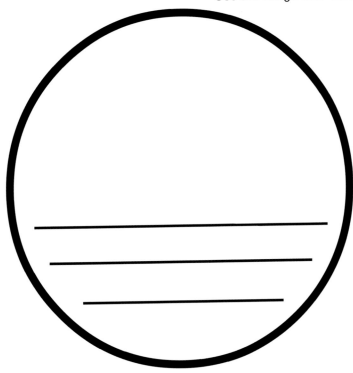

©The Education Center, Inc. • *JUNE, JULY, & AUGUST* • TEC759

Certificate

Use the certificate with "A-camping We Will Go!" on page 15.

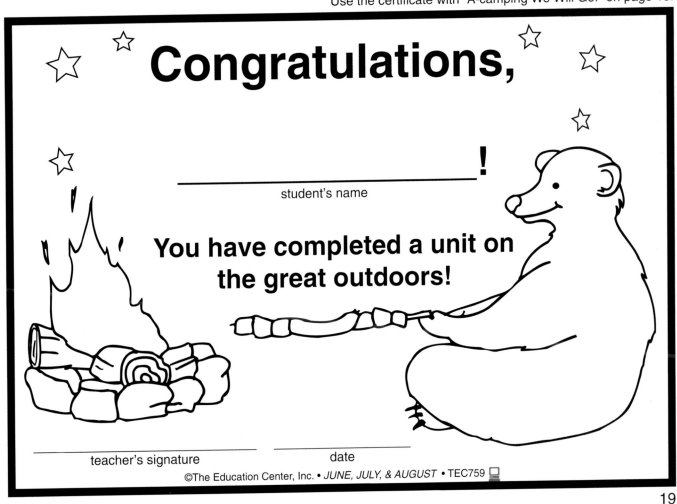

Congratulations,

_____!

student's name

You have completed a unit on the great outdoors!

_____   _____
teacher's signature   date

©The Education Center, Inc. • *JUNE, JULY, & AUGUST* • TEC759

Hip, Hip, Hooray for the USA!

**Strike up the band and step to the beat
of American pride to celebrate patriotic days.**

America the Beautiful
Developing a sense of country

Here's an activity that appeals not only to the eyes but also to the ears. Share the story *America the Beautiful* based on the poem by Katharine Lee Bates and illustrated by Neil Waldman. Display photos, posters, or postcards from America's national parks or other scenic landscapes.

Next, provide each student with a sheet of white construction paper. Have each student draw a picture of her favorite scene from America on her paper. Encourage each child to label her picture. Stimulate students' creativity by playing a recording of "America the Beautiful" or "This Land Is Your Land" while children are working. Bind students' pictures into a classroom collection titled "America the Beautiful."

Stars and Stripes Forever 🖥
Recognizing a commemorative holiday, identifying characteristics of a national symbol

Celebrate Flag Day, June 14, with this "hand-some" activity. Have each student trace his hand on red paper. Instruct him to cut out his shape; then glue the hand cutout to white bulletin board paper as shown. Then provide a group of students with sponges and dark blue tempera paint. Have the group sponge-paint the square in the upper left-hand corner. After the paint has dried, have each student glue on a star that he has cut from white paper. (Provide an accurate, full-color picture of the U.S. flag near your project so students can refer to it for star placement.) Repeat this process until the square has 50 stars on it. Display the resulting flag in the school lobby for all to see.

Hooray for Independence Day!
Building knowledge about a national holiday

Help your youngsters review the history of Independence Day with these sparkling facts. Each year on July Fourth we celebrate our country's birthday. This day is also known as Independence Day.

Independence Day commemorates the signing of the Declaration of Independence on July 4, 1776. Until that time, the colonies in North America were ruled by the king of England. The colonists were becoming more and more unhappy about being under English rule, especially when the king ordered that they pay taxes without representation.

The colonists decided to fight for their freedom. In April of 1775, the king sent troops to take over a supply of the colonists' weapons. But the colonists fought back, and on July 2, 1776, they voted to become an independent nation. When they signed the Declaration of Independence two days later, the United States of America was born! Today we celebrate this patriotic event with parades, picnics, and fireworks displays.

Fun Fourth Fiction
Students will enjoy these fun fourth stories that are bursting with visual appeal!

Celebration!
by Jane Resh Thomas

Happy Birthday, America!
by Marsha Wilson Chall

Hurray for the Fourth of July
by Wendy Watson

Veteran's Day Memories
Learning about a commemorative holiday, showing respect for the contributions of others

Share *The Wall* by Eve Bunting with students. In this moving story, a young boy and his father visit the Vietnam Veterans Memorial in Washington, DC, to find the name of the young boy's grandfather, who was killed in the conflict. After reading the story, ask students if they know anyone who has served in the military or who has given his or her life fighting for our country.

Then honor members of the military and/or veterans with a Veteran's Day tea. Invite one or more veterans or service members to visit your classroom. Encourage students to ask the guests questions such as the following: How long have you served [did you serve] in the military? What was your job in the military? Where were you stationed? What do you remember the most about the time that you served? If possible, snap some photos of the students with the guest(s). For a follow-up activity, have students write reports about their interviews with the guest(s). Mount the photos next to the reports on a bulletin board titled "Our American Heroes."

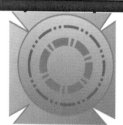

Star-Spangled Cake
Recognizing a national symbol, describing appropriate flag etiquette

Old Glory has never tasted so good! Plan to serve this cake at the Veteran's Day tea or for a patriotic snack any day. Prepare a cake mix, following the directions on the package. Bake as indicated. When the cake has cooled, frost it with white icing. Use blueberries and sliced strawberries to decorate the cake as shown. Ask students to describe ways in which Americans care for and show respect for the American flag. Then serve the cake!

Hip, Hip, Hooray for the USA!

The Birth of Memorial Day 🖥
Building knowledge about a commemorative holiday, developing an awareness of the past

Read the book *Memorial Day* by Helen Frost to help students understand the origins of this holiday. Share the following information with students:

— Memorial Day pays tribute to those who have died while serving our country. It began as a way to honor soldiers who had died in the Civil War.
— On May 5, 1866, one of the first memorials to honor soldiers who gave their lives in the Civil War was held. People in Waterloo, New York, marked the day by closing businesses and stores. They flew their flags at half-mast and decorated soldiers' graves with flags, ribbons, and flowers.
— A Joint Resolution of Congress recognizes Waterloo, New York, as "The Birthplace of Memorial Day."
— In 1971 a law was passed making Memorial Day a federal holiday. Memorial Day is now celebrated on the last Monday in May.
— Poppies came to symbolize fallen soldiers after World War I.

Then have students plan a Memorial Day as it was celebrated years ago. On the day of your celebration, encourage students to dress like students of 1866. Then have your children parade through other classrooms carrying student-made flags and singing songs such as "The Battle Hymn of the Republic" and "The Star-Spangled Banner." Have students read Memorial Day–related poems or stories that they have written (see page 24 for a poetry idea). Inform parents and other relatives about the celebration so that they can plan on attending.

Poppy Day
Showing respect for the contributions of others

Poppy Day—a day on which poppies are sold by veterans' organizations in order to raise money for disabled veterans—is also celebrated on Memorial Day. Let students make their own poppies to present to veterans or enlisted men and women serving in our armed forces. Each student will need three three-inch red tissue paper circles, scissors, and a green pipe cleaner. Instruct each student to stack the tissue paper circles on top of one another. Have each student use her scissors to carefully poke two holes near the center of the circles. Push one end of the pipe cleaner up through one hole, bend it, and bring it down through the other hole. Twist the pipe cleaner to make a stem. Gently fold the tissue paper circles to the center; then unfold them and smooth the petals.

Uncle Sam Wants You!
Learning about a well-known symbol of the United States

Share the story *Casey Over There* by Staton Rabin. This beautiful story is about a young boy named Aubrey whose brother Casey is overseas fighting in World War I. The two communicate back and forth through letters. At one point, however, Aubrey becomes so worried about his brother that he writes a letter to Uncle Sam asking him to let his brother come home. To Aubrey's surprise, he receives a letter—not from Uncle Sam but from President Woodrow Wilson!

Explain that Uncle Sam is a fictional character. Many people think that the original Uncle Sam was a man named Sam Wilson. Wilson inspected meat for our army during the War of 1812 and stamped it with the letters *U.S.* People joked that the meat came from Uncle Sam, and the familiar character we know today was born.

Let students make Uncle Sam craft projects. Each student will need a 3 1/2-inch white construction paper circle, a 4 1/2" x 6" white construction paper rectangle, scissors, glue, crayons, cotton balls, and a copy of the patterns on page 25. Have each student color and cut out her patterns. Then instruct each student to glue her hat to the construction paper circle. Next, glue the jacket behind the construction paper circle. Have each student color her construction paper rectangle as shown to resemble pants; then glue the pants behind the jacket. Next, have each student glue the gloves and shoes as shown. Finish the project by gluing the cotton balls to the face; then add facial features with a black crayon.

Display these projects on a bulletin board with a stars-and-stripes border. Add the title "Uncle Sam Wants You!"

Soldier
Brave, courageous
Marching, saluting, remembering
Proud, honorable
Fighter

Patriotic Poetry 🖥
Identifying characteristics of patriotism, writing poetry

Inspire students to write poems to capture the essence of patriotism. Brainstorm and list on the board words that remind students of patriotic characteristics. (Examples may include *bravery, soldier, courage, freedom, proud,* and *honor.*) Then have students use this list to help them write *diamante* (diamond-shaped) poems following this format:

Line 1: Noun that names the subject
Line 2: Two adjectives
Line 3: Three action verbs ending in *ing*
Line 4: Two adjectives
Line 5: Noun that renames the subject

Name_____

Flag-Waving Facts

Directions:
1. Read the paragraphs below.
2. Cut out the flags at the bottom of the page.
3. Read the information on each rectangle.
4. Place a TRUE flag on each true statement.
5. Place a FALSE flag on each false statement.
6. Put a drop of glue on each dot; then glue the flags in place.

The United States flag is a symbol of America. Our flag has 13 stripes. Each stripe stands for one of the original 13 colonies. There are 50 stars on our flag. Each star represents a state. Our flag is red, white, and blue. The color *red* stands for courage. *White* stands for liberty. *Blue* stands for freedom and justice. Many people believe that Betsy Ross sewed the first flag. There is no proof that this legend is true.

The American flag should be treated with care. The flag should never touch the ground. When a flag becomes dirty, torn, or faded, it should be burned in private.

•	•	•	•
Our flag has 50 stars.	Betsy Ross sewed the first flag.	Each star on the flag stands for a state.	It is okay for the flag to touch the ground.

•	•	•	•
Our flag has 13 stripes.	Each stripe on the flag stands for 1 of the original 13 colonies.	A flag should never be burned.	Each color on the flag has a special meaning.

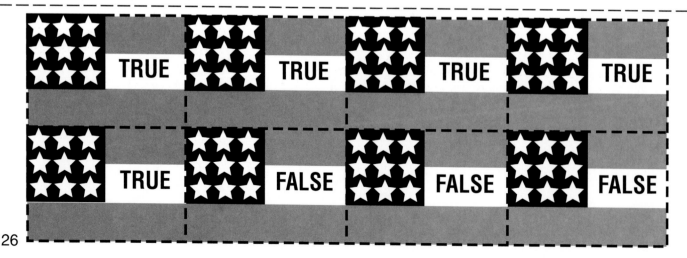

INCREDIBLE INSECTS

Give your students an insight into insects with these fascinating facts and thematic activities. Even if you're squeamish by nature, after doing these activities, you'll have a soft spot for these creepy, sometimes crawly, creatures!

ideas by Cynthia Holcomb

All Kinds of Crawlies
Building background knowledge

They live on the forest floor, on mountaintops, and in open fields. They fly in the air, they crawl on the ground, and they may bug you—but are they all insects? To begin your insect unit, share the following information about insects with your students:

- Insects have three body divisions: the head, the thorax, and the abdomen.
- The head bears the antennae, eyes, and mouthparts.
- The thorax bears the legs and wings. Adult insects have six legs, and many adults have wings.
- The abdomen, the last division, contains sensory organs.
- Insects have an external skeleton (or exoskeleton) that is coated with a waxy layer to help them conserve body moisture.
- Insects are cold-blooded. A chilled insect may have a pulse rate of only one beat per minute, while an active insect may have 140 beats per minute.
- Insects usually breathe by taking in air through a series of holes along the thorax and abdomen.
- Insects smell mostly with their antennae, or feelers.
- Many insects hear through eardrums on their legs or sides, or through the hairs on their bodies.
- Most insects live short lives. Some adult insects only live a few hours.

Buggy Lotto
Recognizing insects

Scientists have identified nearly 1 million kinds of insects, and it is believed that there may be several million that have yet to be discovered. Use the lotto game on page 33 to introduce your students to just a few of these fascinating creatures. To begin, have each student color and cut out the insects and then randomly glue them on the gameboard. As students are programming their gameboards, cut apart the insects on an extra copy of the reproducible. Store the cutouts in a container. Also give several paper markers to each child. To play the game, announce the type of game to be played, such as three in a row or four corners. Then draw an insect from the container and announce its name. Each student covers the announced insect on his board. If desired, have the winner of the first game become the caller of the second game, and so on. Ready to go buggy?

Many Types of Homes
Identifying natural habitats, communicating observations

Give students a firsthand look at where insects live by taking them on a nature walk around your school. If possible, have students explore areas with bushes, trees, grass, dirt, flowers, pavement, and water. Ask students to identify the types of insects in each area while you list their findings in a notebook. Point out that some insects, such as ladybugs and flies, find homes, while others, such as ants and bees, build homes. Back in the classroom, copy the findings onto the chalkboard and initiate a discussion about the types of insects found in each habitat. Ask students to surmise why each insect lives where it does. (Answers may include needs for food, camouflage, and protection.) Then have each student draw one of the habitats and an insect that lives there. Display the illustrations on a bulletin board titled "At Home With Insects."

Insect Hotels
Recognizing basic needs, communicating observations

Now that your youngsters know some facts about insects and their habitats, have them make insect hotels to observe these creatures at close range. For this activity each child needs a clean, half-gallon cardboard milk carton; a light-colored nylon stocking; a twist-tie; and a craft stick or plastic spoon. Help each student cut a rectangle from two opposite sides of the carton and then staple the top closed. Then have him slide the stocking onto the bottom of his carton.

Take your students outdoors and ask each student to collect grass, twigs, a small rock, and soil to place in his carton. Then provide time for the student to find an insect to reside in his hotel. (Have students use the craft sticks or spoons as digging tools.) After he places the insect in the carton, he slides the stocking over the rest of the carton and secures the top of the stocking with the twist-tie. Back in the classroom, have the students use hand lenses to observe the insects. Ask each student to draw a picture of the insect in his hotel and write a description of his insect's activities. After everyone has completed the activity, take the students back outdoors so they may return the bugs to the areas in which they were found.

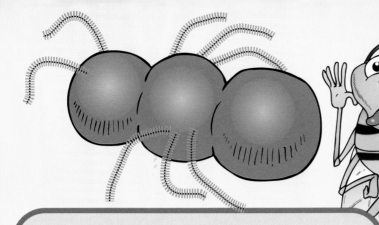

Model Insects 🖥

Identifying the basic parts of an insect

All insects have three body parts: the *head*—where the eyes, two antennae, and mouthparts are found; the *thorax*—where six legs and the wings are attached; and the *abdomen*—where food is digested and eggs are produced. To reinforce the concept of insect body parts, have each student make an insect from clay. Each student will need some modeling clay, one-half of a coffee-stirring stick, and eight short lengths of pipe cleaner. To make an insect, the child divides her clay into three pieces and rolls each piece into a ball. She pushes the balls onto the stirring stick to make the three body parts: the head, thorax, and abdomen. Then she inserts six short lengths of pipe cleaner into the center ball to create the insect's legs. Finally, she adds two pipe cleaner antennae to complete her model insect.

The Good, the Bad, and the Ugly

Understanding how insects interact with their environment

Some insects are harmful. They bite people, they carry germs, or they destroy crops. But other insects are helpful because they carry pollen to help plants reproduce; they serve as food for fish, birds, and many other animals; they eat harmful insects; and they provide us with honey and other products. In fact, many people also eat insects. In South Africa, some people roast termites and eat them by the handfuls, like popcorn. Some stores in the United States sell fried caterpillars and chocolate-covered bees and ants.

After sharing this information, use the word-search puzzle on page 34 to help students identify which insects are helpful to man and which ones cause harm. If desired, serve students a tasty snack of chocolate-covered raisins (ants) while they are working. When students have completed the activity, challenge them to work in small groups to find out additional information about these insects. To do this, divide students into small groups and assign each group three insects listed on the reproducible. Instruct each group to research its insects in the encyclopedia or another reference book and write down at least two facts about each one. Provide time for each group to share its findings with the class. No doubt your students will be buggy with information!

Clevell Harris

The Circle of Life 💻

Comparing insect life cycles, sequencing the stages of a life cycle

Insects have a fascinating life cycle. They come from eggs. The immature insects grow into adults in a series of steps called *metamorphosis*. There are two types of metamorphosis: incomplete and complete. *Incomplete metamorphosis* has three stages: egg, nymph, and adult. These insects bear young that, after hatching from the egg, look very similar to the adult insect. Crickets and dragonflies go through this change. But about 85 percent of insects bear young that, after hatching from the egg, do not resemble the adult in the species. These insects go through *complete metamorphosis:* a four-step development that includes egg, larva, pupa, and adult. Bees, butterflies, and ants go through this change.

After sharing this information with students, have each student make a bracelet to demonstrate his knowledge of a monarch butterfly's life cycle (an example of complete metamorphosis). To do this, a student colors and cuts out a copy of the four stages on page 35. Next, he glues the stages in sequential order to a 2" x 9" construction paper strip. Assist each student in gluing the ends of the strip together to form a bracelet. Then have students don their life-cycle bracelets and discuss each stage of the life cycle. Your students will certainly see how the circle of life brings many interesting changes!

The butterfly lays her eggs.

A caterpillar, or larva, hatches from each egg.

Winged Wonders 💻

Understanding that insects have different characteristics

At first glance, it is easy to confuse butterflies and moths. Both have large pairs of wings and are known for fluttering through the air. But there are several important differences between these two insects. To explain the distinction to your students, make charts similar to the ones shown. Review the characteristics that differentiate a moth from a butterfly. Then divide the class into two groups to complete the following bulletin board activity.

Assign each group one of the two insects. Have each group member illustrate her assigned insect on a sheet of drawing paper. Make available reference materials with illustrations of the two insects for students to refer to. Also encourage students to use the characteristics on the chart for help. While students are drawing their pictures, cover half of a bulletin board with blue paper and the other half with black paper. Add the title "Beautiful Butterflies" on the blue half and "Magnificent Moths" on the black half. When students have completed their drawings, remind them that usually butterflies fly during the day and moths fly during the night. Then have each student cut out her insect and post it on the corresponding side of the board. If desired, ask students to cut out stars to add to the nighttime scene and flowers and a sun for the daytime scene.

Moths
- have thick, furry bodies
- have feathery antennae
- spread their wings when resting
- fly mostly at dusk or at night
- warm themselves by rapidly flapping their wings
- begin as caterpillars in cocoons

Butterflies
- have slender bodies
- have antennae that widen at the ends and resemble clubs
- fold their wings when resting
- fly mostly during the day
- warm themselves in the sun
- begin as caterpillars in chrysalises

Ben

One ladybug can lay hundreds of eggs.

Lovely Ladybugs
Recalling facts from informational text

Whether they are red, orange, yellow, or black, ladybugs are a sight to see! These amazing insects—which are actually beetles—are plenty interesting. The book *Ladybugology* by Michael Elsohn Ross is a fun way to introduce students to these amazing critters. Filled with basic facts, entertaining tidbits, experiments, folklore, and a glossary, this delightful book is sure to spread knowledge about these ever-so-interesting insects.

After reading the book aloud, have each student record facts about ladybugs in a ladybug-shaped booklet. To begin, give a red construction paper copy of the ladybug pattern on page 35 to each student. The student cuts out the pattern and then staples five pieces of white paper behind the cutout. Next, he trims the excess white paper and uses a black marker to personalize the cover. He then folds up the cover and writes a ladybug fact on each sheet of white paper. Pin the completed booklets on a bulletin board titled "Learn About Ladybugs." Invite students and classroom visitors to lift the top page of each booklet to learn about ladybugs.

The "Ant-ics" of Ants
Building background knowledge

Ants play a starring role in *The Magic School Bus® Gets Ants in Its Pants* by Joanna Cole. As Mrs. Frizzle's class makes a video about ants, they follow the starring creature to an anthill and witness ants in action! The characters observe the different jobs in an ant colony, explore the chambers inside an anthill, and get a crash course in ant behavior. The story ends with a hands-on project for your students to try at home. After reading the story aloud, share these amazing ant facts with your students:

- Ants are the most numerous creatures on earth.
- Ants live longer than any other insect—an average of eight years.
- Ants can lift up to 50 times their own weight. That would be like a human lifting two small cars!
- Ants use their antennae for smelling, feeling, detecting vibrations, and even telling the temperature.
- The only places on earth without ants are the polar regions.
- Ants have been on earth since before the days of the dinosaurs.

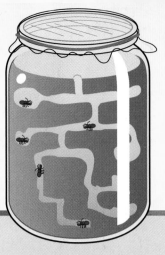

Ants, Bees, and Colonies
Observing insect behavior

What do ants, bees, and the signers of the Declaration of Independence have in common? They're from colonies! Ants and bees are *social* insects, meaning that they live and work together in a colony that is centered around a queen. There are different jobs and castes within the colony. In honey-bee colonies, there are scouts, guards, and attendants to the queen. There are bees called fanners that beat their wings to push air through the hive. There are undertaker bees that remove bodies of dead bees from the hive. In an ant colony, there are soldiers, food foragers, and "nursery" workers that tend to the larvae. All these insects work together in their colonies to help each other.

Provide your students with the opportunity to observe a colony in a *formicarium:* an ant farm. Purchase one at your local science store, keeping in mind that you usually have to order the ants by mail. Or enlist your students' help in making an ant farm from a large, widemouthed jar. To begin, fill the jar with sifted dirt; then collect several ants and place them in the jar. Cover the top of the jar with a piece of nylon stocking secured with a rubber band. Carefully place the jar in a large paper bag as the ants settle into the new environment. Periodically remove the jar from the bag and allow the students to observe the tiny creatures. About every third day, have a student volunteer use an eye-dropper to add about a teaspoon of water to the jar. Also provide the ants with a small amount of jelly or fruit puree once a week. When you culminate your study of insects, return the ants to their natural habitat.

A Bug's-Eye View
Showing an understanding of perspective through artwork

Have your students look at the world from a bug's-eye view! Share the simple story *If I Were an Ant* by Amy Moses with your class. Discuss the comparisons described on each page. Then challenge students to create comparisons using classroom objects. What would an eraser look like to an insect? What would a desk appear to be? On a sheet of drawing paper, have each student describe and illustrate a classroom object from a chosen insect's perspective. Then compile the completed pages in a classroom book titled "If We Were Insects." Let each student have an opportunity to take the book home overnight to share with family and friends.

A pencil would look like a rocket to a cricket.

Go Buggy With Books!

Celebrate your study of incredible insects with this buggy collection of books!

How to Hide a Butterfly: And Other Insects
by Ruth Heller

Bugs and Other Insects
by Bobbie Kalman and Tammy Everts

Creepy, Crawly Baby Bugs
by Sandra Markle

The Icky Bug Alphabet Book
by Jerry Pallotta

Name _____

A Buggy Bunch

Color and cut out the insects.
Mix up the cutouts; then glue each one to the gameboard.

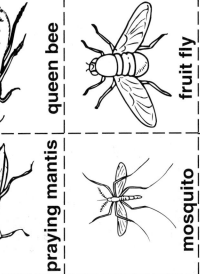

ant

dragonfly

queen bee

fruit fly

ladybug

butterfly

praying mantis

mosquito

termite

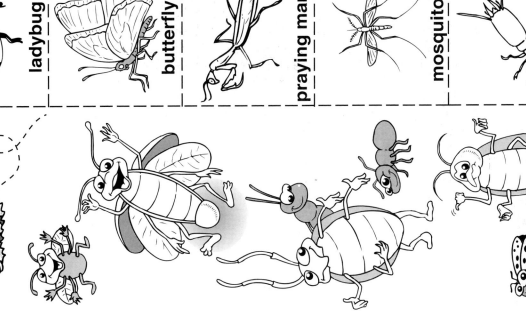

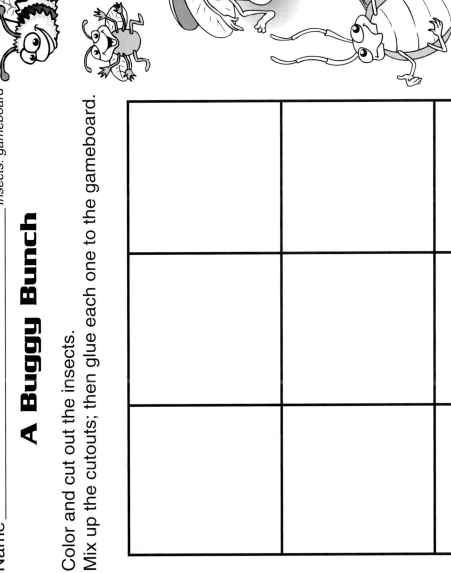

Note to the teacher: Use with "Buggy Lotto" on page 27.

Name _____

All Kinds of Insects

Read about the harmful and helpful insects.
Find their names in the puzzle.

Word Bank

Harmful Insects

A **cockroach** can carry germs.

A **grasshopper** can eat and destroy plants.

A **mosquito** bites people and can carry diseases.

A **flea** bites people and animals.

A **termite** eats wood and can damage houses.

Helpful Insects

A **ladybug** eats harmful insects.

A **dragonfly** eats mosquitoes.

A **bee** makes honey for us to eat.

A **butterfly** spreads pollen to help plants reproduce.

A **silkworm** makes silk for our clothing.

B	D	E	F	G	E	U	O	T	T	C	B	T	R
C	O	C	K	R	O	A	C	H	K	R	U	P	S
L	W	N	L	A	D	Y	B	U	G	N	T	U	I
M	P	X	U	S	A	E	J	R	V	P	T	H	L
O	L	M	O	S	Q	U	I	T	O	F	E	C	K
U	S	W	S	H	E	W	F	Q	R	K	R	M	W
D	R	A	G	O	N	F	L	Y	N	B	F	C	O
Y	I	E	Z	P	K	U	E	M	G	H	L	F	R
B	E	E	F	P	J	R	A	E	W	F	Y	D	M
M	N	L	R	E	W	Q	F	C	N	M	S	L	Y
P	U	T	E	R	M	I	T	E	U	F	D	E	W

Note to the teacher: Use with "The Good, the Bad, and the Ugly" on page 29.

| The butterfly lays her eggs. | A caterpillar, or *larva,* hatches from each egg. | The larva makes a chrysalis (or *pupa*). | The adult butterfly comes out of the chrysalis. |

Ladybug Pattern
Use with "Lovely Ladybugs" on page 31.

A Watermelon Welcome

"Rind" up for a new school year and get off to a rolling start with this thematic unit on everyone's summertime favorite—watermelons!

ideas by Stacie Stone Davis and Lisa Kelly

What a Melon! 💻
Identifying adjectives, communicating observations

Here's a nifty way to start the school year! Prior to the start of school, collect the names and addresses of your future students. Copy the letter shown onto the watermelon pattern on page 42; then make student copies. Personalize the letters and mail them to your students. When the first day of school arrives, place a large watermelon atop a table in a prominent classroom location. Invite students to each use a permanent marker to write adjectives describing this juicy melon on the watermelon. Then slice the watermelon, provide each student with a sample, and discuss with students their reactions to the food. My, what a tasty first day of school it was!

Dear _____,

I am looking forward to meeting you on the first day of school. I have some special activities planned for us! All of the activities will have to do with a juicy summer food. The food is green on the outside and pink on the inside. It has lots of seeds inside too. It's very juicy! Can you rearrange the letters below to spell the name of the mystery food? See you soon!

From,

_____

It's a _ _ _ _ _ _ _ _ _ _ _ !

(MNOEATWRLE)

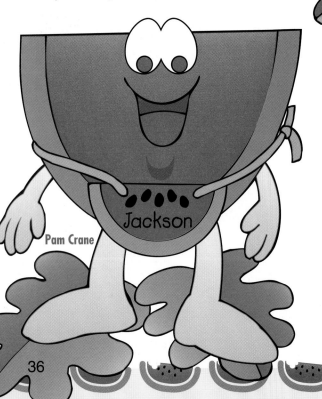

Jackson

Pam Crane

Watermelon Nametags
Introducing and speaking about oneself

This neat nametag project doubles as a getting-to-know-you activity. To make a nametag, a child glues a pink or red construction paper semicircle atop a slightly larger green construction paper semicircle as shown. He uses a black crayon to personalize his watermelon half and then glues a desired number of clean watermelon seeds (or construction paper seeds) to the nametag. Next, he punches two holes at the top of his nametag. Finally, he threads a length of yarn through the holes, ties the yarn ends, and wears the nametag around his neck.

After students have completed the projects, gather them in a large circle on the floor. Encourage each child to introduce himself; then, for each seed that is glued to his nametag, ask the child to share a fact about himself. No doubt students will enjoy this appetizing activity!

Who Me?

Melon Patch Fun

Participating in rhyme, developing a class community

This enjoyable game is perfect for helping students learn each other's names at the beginning of the school year. As children become increasingly confident with the rhyme, challenge them to add a clap and a snap movement while they are chanting.

Who Took the Melon From the Melon Patch?

(chanted to the rhythm of "Who Stole the Cookies From the Cookie Jar?")

All: Who took the melon from the melon patch?
Leader: [Student's name] took the melon from the melon patch.
Student named: Who me?
All: Yes, you!
Student named: Couldn't be!
All: Then who?

Student named: [Another student's name] took the melon from the melon patch.
Second student named: Who me?
All: Yes, you!
Second student named: Couldn't be!
All: Then who?

Repeat the rhyme in this same manner until each student has had a chance to be named. The last person called is "in the melon patch" and starts the game as the leader the next time it is played.

Juicy Jobs

Demonstrating responsible behavior

Looking for a great way to grow a crop of responsible students? Try this deliciously easy idea! From bulletin board paper, cut a large watermelon shape and mount it on a bulletin board. Also cut several seed shapes from black construction paper and attach those to the watermelon. Print the name of a classroom job—such as line leader, messenger, a caboose—above each seed cutout. Next, have each student draw a likeness of herself on a piece of white construction paper (smaller than the seed cutout). Or, if desired, take a photograph of each child. Laminate the drawings or photographs; then store them in a resealable plastic bag pinned to the bulletin board. When you're ready to assign jobs, simply pin a student's drawn picture or photo atop the black seed cutout bearing the name of the job that the student will perform.

Juicy Jobs

Messenger

Line Leader

Zookeeper

A Patch of Graphing Practice

Using prior knowledge, interpreting data

Sweeten your students' graphing skills with this daily activity. Reduce a copy of the watermelon pattern (page 42) to 50 percent. Then make student copies on white construction paper. Have each student color, personalize, and cut out her watermelon pattern. Laminate the watermelon cutouts for durability and store them in a container near the chalkboard. Then, each morning, write a watermelon-related fact on the board (see the provided list) and the words "true" and "false" below it in two columns. When each student arrives, have her read the fact, decide whether she thinks the statement is true or false, and then tape her watermelon cutout in the appropriate column. Before the end of the day, analyze the data collected before revealing the answer.

True Watermelon Facts

- Egyptians grew watermelons more than 5,000 years ago; wall paintings were decorated with them.
- Watermelons are about 93 percent water.
- Most watermelons weigh from five to 40 pounds.
- Some watermelons weigh up to 100 pounds.
- Watermelons grow on vines.
- As many as 15 watermelons may grow on one vine.
- In some places watermelons are fed to farm animals.
- Watermelons are considered as vegetables by horticulturists.
- A ripe watermelon makes a hollow thud when thumped.
- Every part of the watermelon may be eaten.

The Scoop on Watermelons

Identifying characteristics of plants, reciting a chant

Most people think that watermelon is a fruit. Actually, because it grows on a vine and must be replanted annually, horticulturists consider it to be a vegetable. It belongs to the gourd family, which includes squash, pumpkins, and cucumbers. Just like many other plants, a watermelon's roots grow underground and its vine acts as a stem. After sharing this information with your students, invite them to join you in the following chant.

The Watermelon Chant

(chanted to the rhythm of "Peanut, Peanut Butter")

Chorus:
Water, watermelon—*(whisper)* tastes great.
Water, watermelon—*(whisper)* tastes great.

Verses:
First you plant a seed and it grows. It grows.
It really, really grows.
Pretend to plant a seed.

Then you pick the melon. You pick it. You pick it.
You really, really pick it.
Pretend to pick a watermelon.

Now it's time to slice it, to slice it.
You really, really slice it.
Pretend to slice a melon.

Then it's time to eat it, to eat it.
You really, really eat it.
Pretend to eat watermelon.

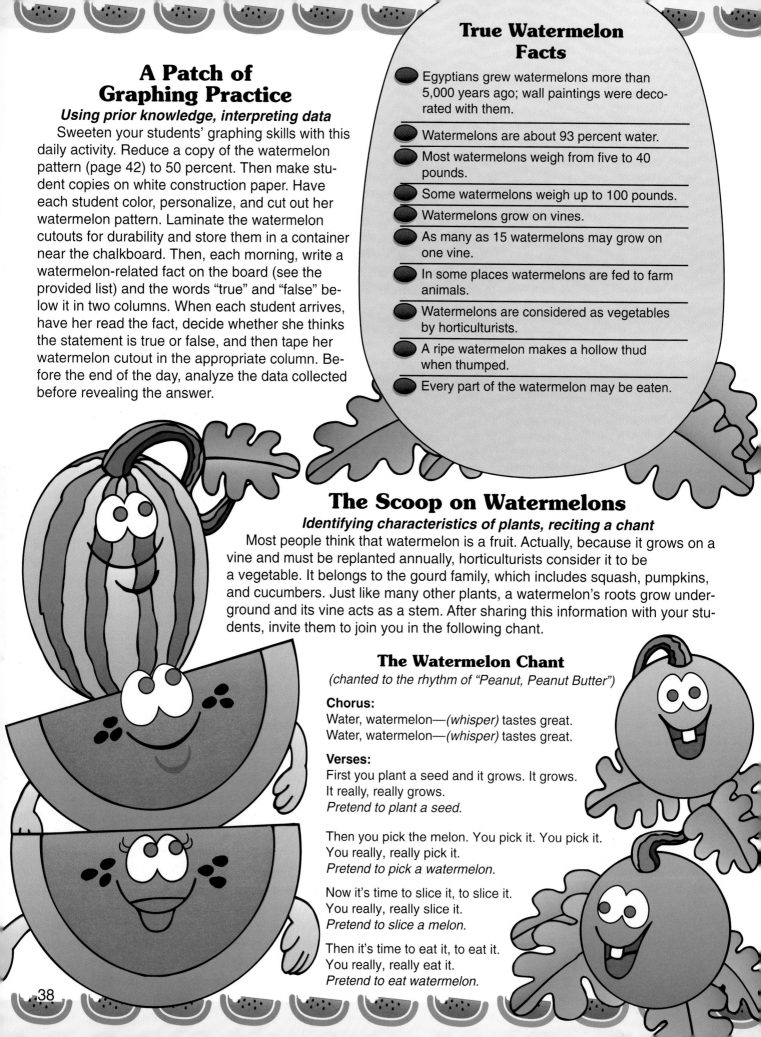

Once upon a time, a little _____

1

went into a watermelon patch. He couldn't believe his eyes! Before him was a large

_____ watermelon that

2

weighed at least _____ pounds.

3

The tiny critter _____ to the

4

watermelon and tried to lift it, but it wouldn't budge. So the little critter decided to eat the watermelon. He ate it in

_____ bite(s)!

5

Wacky Tales From the Watermelon Patch

Following directions, illustrating to show comprehension

Here's a wacky way to spur on some watermelon-related tales! To begin, have each student number a sheet of lined paper from 1 to 5. Then read aloud the descriptions below. For each description, the student writes a word or a numeral on his paper.

1. the name of a small animal
2. a color
3. a large number
4. a past tense action verb
5. a number less than ten

Afterward, give each child a copy of a story frame like the one shown. Instruct each child to copy the words from his lined paper onto the corresponding story blanks. Then encourage each student to draw a corresponding illustration for his story. Invite students to share these wacky tales with their classmates. If desired, have students rewrite their stories on special watermelon writing paper (see "Sweet Stationery").

Sweet Stationery

Demonstrating an art technique

The idea of writing on this pretty paper will have your pupils penning poem after poem, story after story. To make the stationery, students will need sheets of white construction paper, pink or red tempera paint, sponges that have been cut into semicircles, and green and black felt-tip pens. First, have each student dip a sponge shape into the paint and then gently press the sponge onto the construction paper to create a watermelon border. After the paint has dried, ask each student to use a green felt-tip pen to add watermelon rinds. To complete the project, have him use a black pen to draw watermelon seeds. Encourage students to use the paper to publish watermelon-related tales, poems, or letters.

A Perfect Patch

Reading independently for pleasure

Any way you slice it, this display is sure to whet your students' appetites for reading. Give each child a white construction paper copy of the watermelon pattern on page 42. Each student personalizes the rind and then colors it green. Next, he sponge-paints the remainder of the watermelon pink. After the projects dry, mount them on a bulletin board titled "A Perfect Patch of Readers." Then, each time a child completes a book, have him glue a black construction paper seed atop his watermelon cutout. When a child earns ten seeds, reward him with a small prize or privilege.

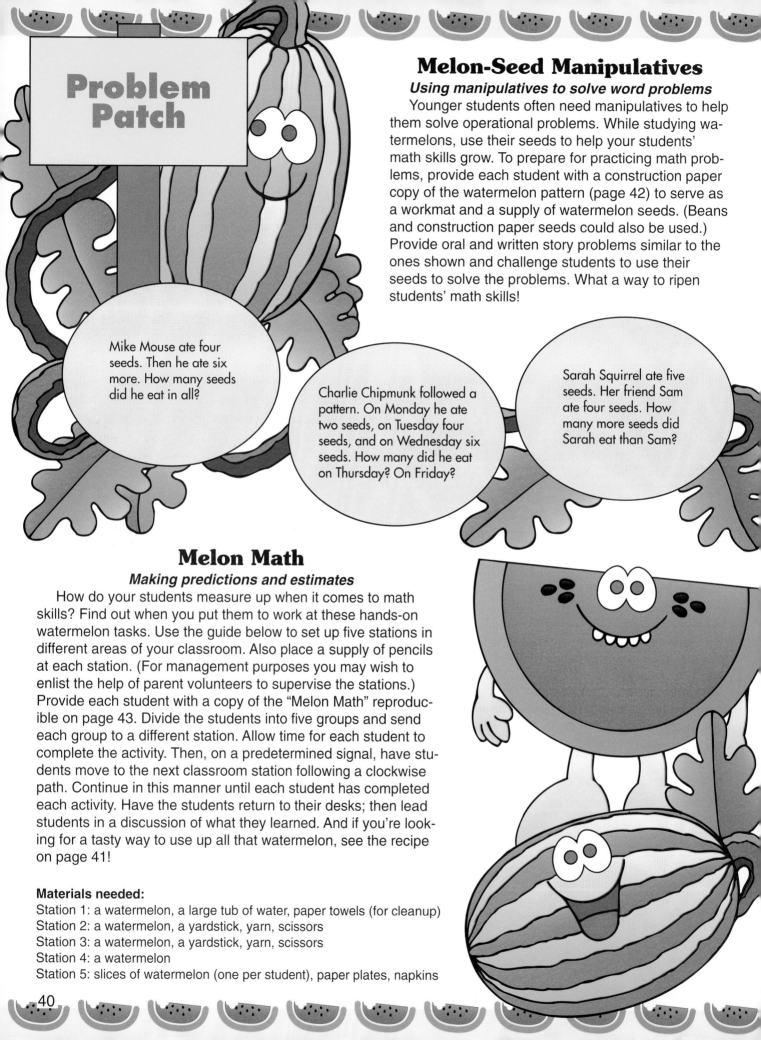

Problem Patch

Melon-Seed Manipulatives
Using manipulatives to solve word problems

Younger students often need manipulatives to help them solve operational problems. While studying watermelons, use their seeds to help your students' math skills grow. To prepare for practicing math problems, provide each student with a construction paper copy of the watermelon pattern (page 42) to serve as a workmat and a supply of watermelon seeds. (Beans and construction paper seeds could also be used.) Provide oral and written story problems similar to the ones shown and challenge students to use their seeds to solve the problems. What a way to ripen students' math skills!

Mike Mouse ate four seeds. Then he ate six more. How many seeds did he eat in all?

Charlie Chipmunk followed a pattern. On Monday he ate two seeds, on Tuesday four seeds, and on Wednesday six seeds. How many did he eat on Thursday? On Friday?

Sarah Squirrel ate five seeds. Her friend Sam ate four seeds. How many more seeds did Sarah eat than Sam?

Melon Math
Making predictions and estimates

How do your students measure up when it comes to math skills? Find out when you put them to work at these hands-on watermelon tasks. Use the guide below to set up five stations in different areas of your classroom. Also place a supply of pencils at each station. (For management purposes you may wish to enlist the help of parent volunteers to supervise the stations.) Provide each student with a copy of the "Melon Math" reproducible on page 43. Divide the students into five groups and send each group to a different station. Allow time for each student to complete the activity. Then, on a predetermined signal, have students move to the next classroom station following a clockwise path. Continue in this manner until each student has completed each activity. Have the students return to their desks; then lead students in a discussion of what they learned. And if you're looking for a tasty way to use up all that watermelon, see the recipe on page 41!

Materials needed:
Station 1: a watermelon, a large tub of water, paper towels (for cleanup)
Station 2: a watermelon, a yardstick, yarn, scissors
Station 3: a watermelon, a yardstick, yarn, scissors
Station 4: a watermelon
Station 5: slices of watermelon (one per student), paper plates, napkins

Pick-of-the-Patch Literature

Eating the Alphabet: Fruits and Vegetables From A to Z
written and illustrated by Lois Ehlert

Fruit or Vegetable	Color	Texture	Any Seeds?	Firmness
apple	outside: red inside: white	smooth	yes	hard

Communicating observations, making comparisons

"Apple to zucchini, come take a look. Start eating your way through this alphabet book." No doubt your students have tasted watermelon, which is featured in this book. But how many students have heard of—let alone tasted—dates, endive, or kohlrabi? If the answer is zero, invite your students to eat their way through the alphabet. To do this, have each student bring to school a desired fruit or vegetable that is featured in the book. Ask that the food be ready for consumption and that there be enough of the item so that each child may have a small sampling. Then, for each item that is tasted, complete a section of a chart similar to the one shown. To conclude the activity, have students discuss the similarities and differences among the sampled foods.

Chestnut Cove
written and illustrated by Tim Egan
Working cooperatively toward a common goal

Cooperation was a way of life in the friendly town of Chestnut Cove until a watermelon-growing contest threatened to change everything. After sharing this story, discuss with students the meaning of the word *cooperation.* Guide students to understand that cooperation among people is imperative when working toward a common goal. Then divide your students into cooperative groups. Provide each group with potting soil, a watermelon seed, and a container suitable for planting. Encourage each group to work together to plant its seed and, in the following weeks, to continue to nurture the tiny plant. (Be sure to tell students that watermelon seeds will not produce melons when grown indoors, but they will yield vines.) Emphasize the fact that there will be no special prize given to the group with the largest plant. Afterward, discuss the differences in attitude between the Chestnut Cove residents and your students.

Watermelon Day
written by Kathi Appelt
Responding to literature

Jesse finds a special watermelon growing in the corner of her garden. Although she eagerly anticipates eating the watermelon, she realizes she must wait until Watermelon Day when it will be ripe and ready. Lively text and pastel illustrations combine to create a story that celebrates the wonderful pleasures of summer.

To Jesse, Watermelon Day meant cousins and cold peach ice cream, softball and songs. Invite your students to name activities that they would incorporate into their own Watermelon Day festivities. Then, with your students' assistance, plan your own Watermelon Day. When the festivities are over, treat your students to a special snack of watermelon pops.

Watermelon Pops
(Makes 12 three-ounce pops)

Ingredients:
1 can frozen concentrated pink lemonade
4 c. watermelon, cubed and seeded
1 c. ice cubes

Directions:
1. In a blender, mix lemonade and watermelon until well-blended.
2. Add the ice cubes to the blender and pulse until slushy.
3. Pour the mixture into Popsicle® trays and place in the freezer. When the pops are still mushy, insert a Popsicle® stick into each one.

Pattern

Use with "What a Melon!" on page 36, "A Patch of Graphing Practice" on page 38, "A Perfect Patch" on page 39, and "Melon-Seed Manipulatives" on page 40.

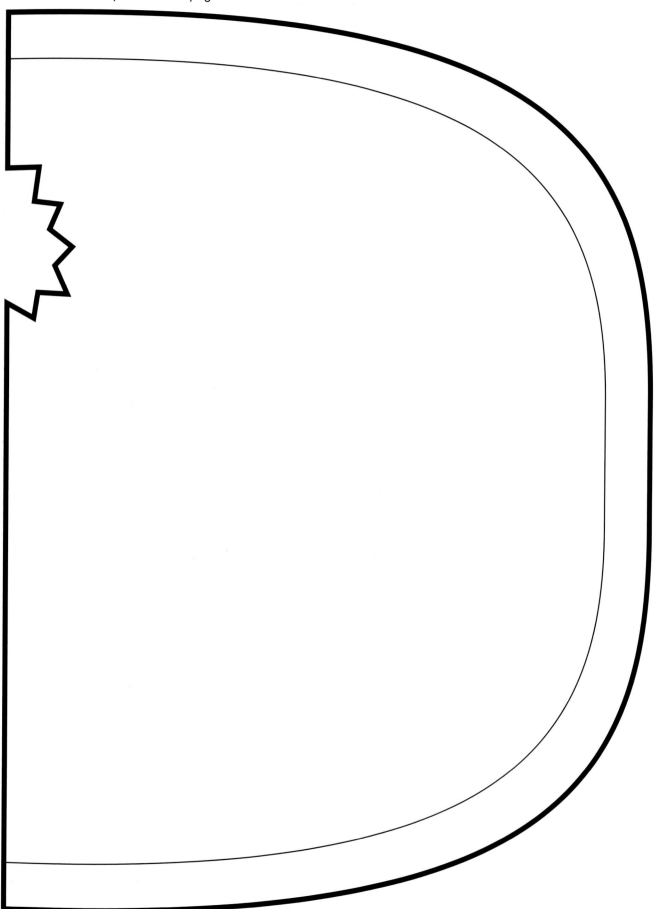

Name _____

Melon Math

Read the question.
Make a guess.
Check.

	Guess	Check
Does the watermelon sink or float? 1. Place the melon in the tub and observe.		
What is the *circumference* of the watermelon? 1. Use the yarn to measure. 2. Straighten the yarn and measure its length with a yardstick.		
What is the *length* of your watermelon? 1. Use the yarn to measure. 2. Measure the yarn's length with a yardstick.		
How many stripes does your watermelon have? 1. Count.		
How many seeds does your watermelon slice have? 1. Count.		

Note to the teacher: Use with "Melon Math" on page 40.

SUMMERTIME TRAVEL

Whether students took a trip to the mountains, traveled to the lake, spent a week at the beach, or enjoyed the lazy days of summer at home, summer vacation is sure to have generated excitement amongst your youngsters. Have your students grab their suitcases full of memories and unpack them for this learning adventure!

ideas by Darcy Brown, Lisa Buchholz, and Heather E. Graley

SUITCASE SOUVENIRS

Telling about personal experiences, locating places on a map

Your young travelers will love reliving their summertime memories when they share treasured vacation mementos with their classmates. In advance, staple a U.S. map to the middle of a bulletin board titled "Summer Travel Tour." Photograph each student and mount the photos around the border of the board. Using a permanent marker, write "Tour Guide" on a self-adhesive label; then attach it to the front of a child-size visor. Ask each youngster to bring from home a small suitcase or duffel bag filled with five items that remind him of a trip he took over the summer. Items might include photographs, brochures, and souvenirs. When the items

have been brought to school, have each student, in turn, wear the visor and share his items with his classmates while keeping the location of his trip a secret. Encourage youngsters to guess the location to which the child traveled. After a student's trip location has been correctly identified, the student attaches a length of yarn from his photo to the location on the map. The student who correctly guessed the location becomes the next tour guide. Let the tours begin!

CREATIVE CARRY-ONS

Identifying needs, sorting by categories

What better way to pack up trip memories than with these creative carry-ons! To make her carry-on, a student stacks two 12" x 18" sheets of construction paper and folds them in half. With the fold at the bottom, she staples the sides of her carry-on together. She then staples the sections together to create two pockets. She cuts a handle from a 3" x 7" strip of construction paper and tapes it to her carry-on. Then she decorates her carry-on as desired. Next, she selects a place she has taken a trip to and brainstorms specific items she took with her, such as appropriate clothing, shampoo, a travel book, and a map. Then she illustrates and labels the items on separate index cards. Challenge each student to sort her cards, by clothing and nonclothing items, into the two pockets of her carry-on. Encourage students to take their carry-ons home to share with their families.

Kimberly Richard

VACATION PONDERINGS
Generating possible answers within a given category

Where are we going? How will we get there? What will we do? When it comes to taking a trip, these questions are often asked by youngsters. Provide time for students to discuss these questions with this cooperative-group activity. Divide students into three groups and give each group a sheet of poster board labeled with one of the questions. Then have each group brainstorm ideas to fill the poster. To do this, each group cuts appropriate pictures from magazines, glues them to the poster, and labels them with markers. When the posters are complete, encourage each group to discuss its poster with the class.

For an added challenge, instruct each youngster to choose a different item from each poster. Have him write a story that incorporates the item he selected and then illustrate it as desired. If time allows, have students share their stories with their classmates.

TOP-NOTCH TRAVEL BROCHURES
Summarizing information

Your youngsters will be eager to share these unique travel brochures with friends and family. Explain that travel brochures inform readers about a particular area or place. Share with students a variety of brochures obtained from a local travel agency. Then have each student create a brochure featuring his summer vacation spot. Make one white construction paper copy of the travel brochure on page 50 for each student. To make his brochure, a student answers the questions with information about his travel destination; then he adds illustrations as noted. He cuts out his brochure and then folds it along the thin lines so that the programming remains on the inside. Then he unfolds the brochure, flips it over, and prints the title "A Trip to [student's destination]" on the far right panel. To finish his brochure, he decorates the two remaining panels with illustrations of his destination before refolding it (making sure the title is on the front). Each day select a few students to share their brochures with their classmates. Heighten the experience by asking youngsters to dress in clothing suitable for their travel destinations and to share some of the items from "Suitcase Souvenirs" on page 44. If desired, challenge students to create commercials of their travel destinations to present to their classmates.

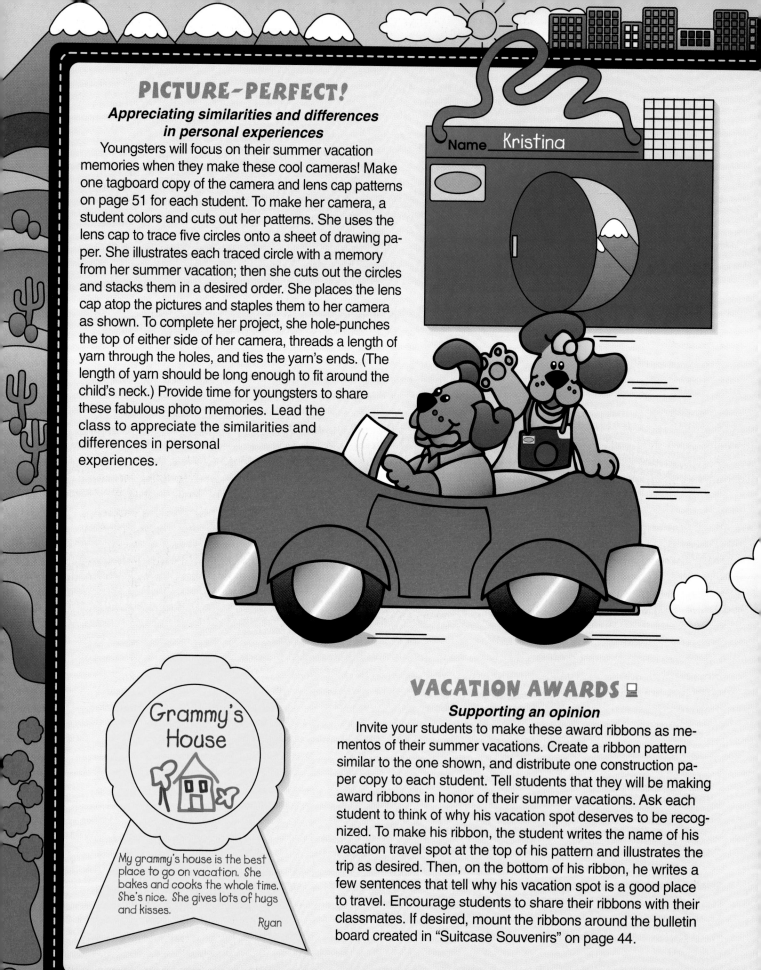

PICTURE-PERFECT!

Appreciating similarities and differences in personal experiences

Youngsters will focus on their summer vacation memories when they make these cool cameras! Make one tagboard copy of the camera and lens cap patterns on page 51 for each student. To make her camera, a student colors and cuts out her patterns. She uses the lens cap to trace five circles onto a sheet of drawing paper. She illustrates each traced circle with a memory from her summer vacation; then she cuts out the circles and stacks them in a desired order. She places the lens cap atop the pictures and staples them to her camera as shown. To complete her project, she hole-punches the top of either side of her camera, threads a length of yarn through the holes, and ties the yarn's ends. (The length of yarn should be long enough to fit around the child's neck.) Provide time for youngsters to share these fabulous photo memories. Lead the class to appreciate the similarities and differences in personal experiences.

Name Kristina

Grammy's House

My grammy's house is the best place to go on vacation. She bakes and cooks the whole time. She's nice. She gives lots of hugs and kisses.

Ryan

VACATION AWARDS

Supporting an opinion

Invite your students to make these award ribbons as mementos of their summer vacations. Create a ribbon pattern similar to the one shown, and distribute one construction paper copy to each student. Tell students that they will be making award ribbons in honor of their summer vacations. Ask each student to think of why his vacation spot deserves to be recognized. To make his ribbon, the student writes the name of his vacation travel spot at the top of his pattern and illustrates the trip as desired. Then, on the bottom of his ribbon, he writes a few sentences that tell why his vacation spot is a good place to travel. Encourage students to share their ribbons with their classmates. If desired, mount the ribbons around the bulletin board created in "Suitcase Souvenirs" on page 44.

MAPPING MILEAGE 🖥

Measuring length, using scale to determine distance

Youngsters will get miles of use out of this center activity! Program each of ten index cards with line segments that can be measured in exact inches (or centimeters). Label each card with a different numeral from 1 to 10. Then program the back of each card with its corresponding answers. Prepare a class supply of a sheet similar to the one shown; then place the cards, the sheets, and a supply of rulers at a center. A student selects a card and measures the line segments with a ruler. She adds the lengths together, writes the length on the provided line, and then flips the card to check her work. She then converts the mileage accordingly. For an added challenge, explain how a car's odometer keeps track of the miles a car has been driven. Then, each day, write down the mileage of your own car and have youngsters find the total number of miles you drove in one week.

GREAT GRIDS!

Using a map grid

Reinforce the concept of using a map grid with this great idea! Explain to your youngsters that map grids provide a helpful way to find places on a map. Many maps are divided into equally sized squares that have numbers along the top and letters down the left side. The coordinates on the map are read by saying the square's letter first and then its number. Next, copy the grid on page 52 for each student. Have each student color and cut out the six travel destinations, read their coordinates, and glue them in the correct squares on the map. For an added challenge, have students research the places on the map and write the names of the cities and states where these famous places can be found.

A SHOPPING CENTER 🖥

Using coin manipulatives to solve word problems

Here's a center activity that reinforces money skills and helps students understand what items need to be packed for a trip. Glue magazine pictures of items needed for travel—such as toothpaste, a toothbrush, and film—to the inside of a file folder. Label the pictures with prices appropriate for your students. Attach an envelope to the outside of the folder. Program index cards with money problems for students to complete that are related to the magazine pictures. Program the back of each card with its corresponding answer, and store the cards in the envelope. Write the directions on the front of the folder; then place the folder and a supply of plastic coins at a center. A student selects a card and uses the plastic coins to complete the problem or activity. Then he flips the card to check his work.

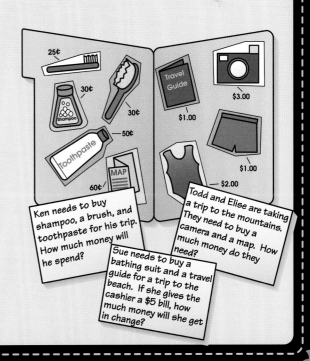

BEACH BALL MADNESS

Answering questions about personal experiences

This exciting game provides youngsters with a unique way to discuss their summer vacations. Use a permanent marker to write questions like "Where did you travel this summer?" and "What sights did you see on your trip?" on different sections of a large beach ball. Next, ask each student to bring to school a beach towel and a pair of sunglasses. Have students sit in a circle on their beach towels while wearing their sunglasses. To play the game, toss the beach ball to a student and have her answer the question her right thumb is touching. Then have her toss the ball to another student and have him repeat the activity. Play continues in this same manner until each student has had a turn. To keep track of students who have taken a turn, have them remove their sunglasses after answering a question.

SUMMERTIME TRAVEL

Conducting a survey

A scavenger hunt is a great way for students to learn a little about one another's summer vacations. Each player needs a copy of the scavenger hunt sheet on page 53. The object of the hunt is for each youngster to obtain as many signatures on his sheet as possible. Students may only sign a grid if the fact is true about themselves. Set a time limit (such as 10 or 15 minutes), and let the hunt begin. When time has expired, have students count the number of signatures they've collected. If desired, select a few students to share one or two interesting details that they have learned about their classmates. Then reward all youngsters with a sticker or another small treat.

TAKE A TRIP TO...

Participating in cooperative play

Engage your youngsters in this terrific travel game (patterned after the popular game Four Corners). As a class, decide on four favorite places students like to take trips, such as the beach, the mountains, Disney World®, and the zoo. Label one corner of your classroom for each destination. Then select a player to be the caller. To begin play, the designated student closes his eyes, calls "Time to travel," and counts to ten aloud. The remaining students quietly walk to one of the four areas. With his eyes still closed, the designated student announces the name of a destination. The students who are at that destination must return to their seats. Play continues in the same manner until only one child remains standing. Reward the winning youngster with a chance to be the caller, and play the game again!

TRAVEL TALES

Take your students on a trip through these terrific travel tales.

Arthur's Family Vacation
by Marc Brown
Writing a prioritized list

When Arthur's family takes a trip to the beach, their plans are spoiled by rain. Young Arthur saves the day by taking his family on a field trip! After reading the story, challenge your students to come up with their own lists of rainy-day activities. As a homework assignment, ask each youngster to write a top ten list of activities his family could do on a rainy day. The next day, have him list his activities on a piece of poster board, starting with 10. He then adds a title similar to the one shown and desired decorations around his list. Provide time for youngsters to share their rainy-day rankings with their classmates.

The Saunders Family's
Top Ten Rainy-Day Activities

10. Play charades.
9. Play a game.
8. Play on the computer.
7. Order a pizza.
6. Rent a movie.
5. Bake cookies.
4. Look at old pictures.
3. Watch home videos.
2. Write a letter to Grammy.
1. Snuggle up and read a good story together.

Stringbean's Trip to the Shining Sea
by Vera B. Williams and Jennifer Williams
Writing and addressing a postcard

Introduce your youngsters to postcard writing with this delightful story. Stringbean and his older brother, Fred, travel across the states one summer sending postcards home to their family. After sharing the postcards with your students, challenge each youngster to write a postcard to a friend or family member describing a trip she took over summer vacation. (Those who didn't go away for a vacation may choose to write about something they did with their families.) On the unlined side of a large index card, ask each student to illustrate her trip. Then she turns the card over and describes the things she saw and did while she was on her trip. Have each student address the postcard and design a colorful postage stamp. Encourage each student to hand-deliver her postcard to a friend or family member.

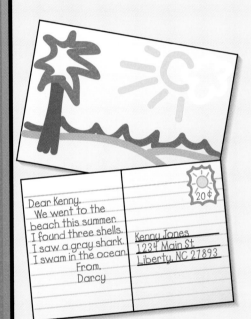

Dear Kenny,
We went to the beach this summer. I found three shells. I saw a gray shark. I swam in the ocean.
From,
Darcy

20¢

Kenny Jones
1234 Main St.
Liberty, NC 27893

Dinosaurs Travel:
A Guide for Families on the Go
by Laurie Krasny Brown and Marc Brown
Applying alphabetic principle, using conventions of writing

Ease the stress associated with travel when you share this unique travel guide packed full of helpful traveling tips. After reading the story aloud, have students create this alphabet book of travel tips. Assign each student a different letter of the alphabet. The student writes her assigned letter at the top of a sheet of story paper; then she writes and illustrates a travel tip that begins with her letter. Collect the pages and arrange them in alphabetical order between two construction paper covers. Then add the title "Travel Tips From *A* to *Z!*" to the front cover.

A
Always buckle your seat belt!

B
Bring your toothbrush and toothpaste.

C
Carry a small bag if you fly on a plane.

D
Don't forget to bring your camera!

50

Travel Brochure

of

What is the place like?

Draw a picture of the place.

What can visitors do?

Draw a picture of something visitors can do.

What sights can visitors see?

Draw a picture of something visitors can see.

Note to the teacher: Use with "Top-Notch Travel Brochures" on page 45.

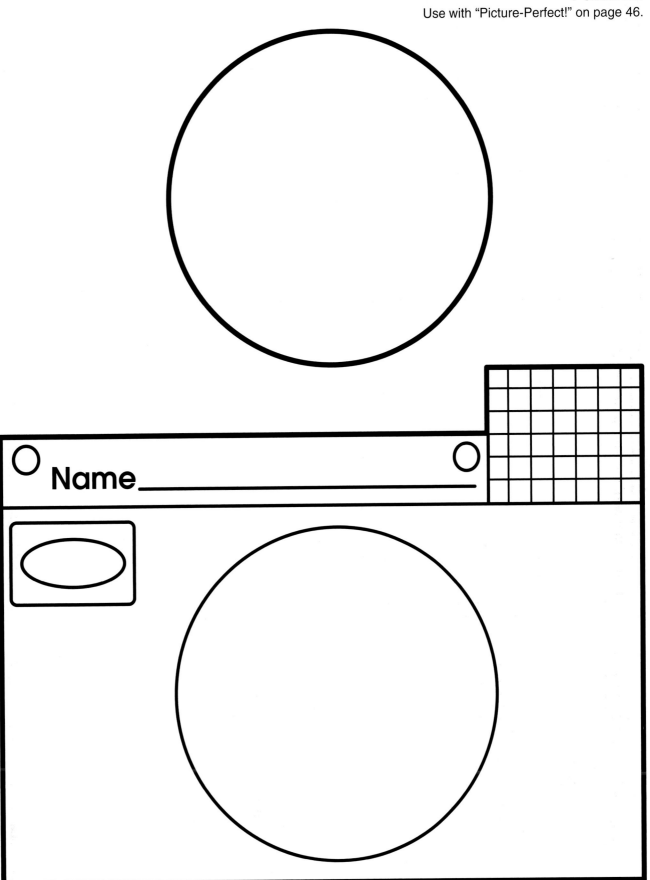

Name_____

52   Name _____

A Great Grid

Cut out the boxes below.
Glue each picture onto its correct coordinate.

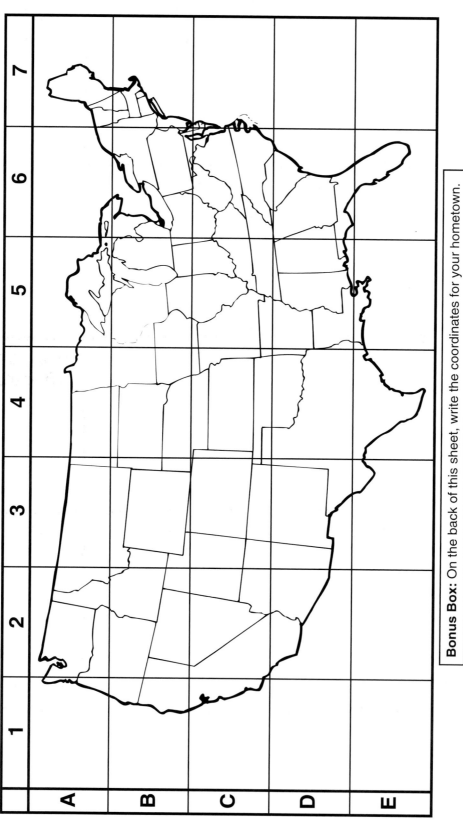

	1	2	3	4	5	6	7
A							
B							
C							
D							
E							

Bonus Box: On the back of this sheet, write the coordinates for your hometown.

©The Education Center, Inc. • *JUNE, JULY, & AUGUST* • TEC759

B7	B3	A2	C1	B5	E6
Statue of Liberty	Mount Rushmore National Memorial	Mount St. Helens	Golden Gate Bridge	The Sears Tower	Disney World®

Note to the teacher: Use with "Great Grids!" on page 47.

Name _____

Summertime Travel Scavenger Hunt

Went swimming	Visited another state	Visited another country	Went to Disney World®
Went camping	Rode on a train	Went fishing	Sat around a campfire
Went to a museum	Took a hike	Rode bikes	Stayed over at a friend's house
Went to camp	Went to the beach	Visited the mountains	Took a boat ride
Went to a county/ state fair	Had a picnic	Took pictures with a camera	Flew on an airplane

Note to the teacher: Use with "Summertime Travel" on page 48.

Meet Kevin Henkes!

Introduce youngsters to author and illustrator Kevin Henkes. His delightful characters and humorous stories will entice students of all ages!

ideas by Darcy Brown

Background for the Teacher
Learning about an author-illustrator

Kevin Henkes was born on November 27, 1960, in Racine, Wisconsin. He began to draw at an early age and liked to read a lot as a child. His first book, *All Alone,* was published by Greenwillow Books in 1981. Since then, Henkes has written more than 20 children's books and novels. One of his most recent picture books, *Lilly's Purple Plastic Purse,* has won several awards, including the *BCCB* Blue Ribbon, the *Boston Globe* Best of 1996, and the NAPPA Gold Award.

One of Greenwillow Books' best-selling children's authors, Henkes attributes his success to the encouragement he received from his parents and teachers. He has often said that he "never thought [he'd] be lucky enough to be a real author and illustra-

tor." And now he wouldn't trade that for anything else in the world!

Owen
Supporting a personal opinion

When Owen's parents tell him he needs to give up his favorite blanket, Owen has other plans. Many of your students may have had experiences similar to Owen's. After reading the story, have your students think of objects they cherish and could never ever part with. Have each student illustrate her object on a six-inch square of white construction paper. Next, have her share her picture and explain why she could never part with the object. Collect the pictures and glue them to a large sheet of yellow bulletin board paper, leaving three inches on the top and bottom edges of the paper. Cut fringe along these edges of the paper as shown. Display the resulting blanket and the title "Things We Could Never Part With" for everyone to enjoy.

Best Wishes, Curtis!

Good-bye, Curtis

Recalling details, making a personal connection

After 42 years of being a letter carrier, Curtis decides to retire. The people along Curtis's route plan a special surprise for his last day of work. Enlist your youngsters' help in creating a special display to commemorate Curtis's service. To prepare, enlarge the mailbox pattern on page 58. Write the title "Our Gifts for Curtis!" on the pattern; then color the mailbox, cut it out, and staple it to a bulletin board.

After reading the story aloud, have youngsters name the gifts Curtis receives. Ask students to discuss gifts they might give to Curtis. Then have each youngster create her special gift. To do this, the student illustrates the desired gift on a four-inch square of tagboard. Next, she staples a four-inch square of wrapping paper atop the tagboard along the top edge. To complete the project, she glues a small ribbon bow atop the staple. After youngsters share their gifts with their classmates, mount the projects on the prepared bulletin board.

For an additional activity, have students design stamps that Curtis would like. To do this, each student illustrates a picture on a copy of the stamp pattern on page 58. Next, she cuts out this pattern and glues it to a slightly larger sheet of construction paper. Mount the completed stamps around the bulletin board. No doubt everybody will *always* love Curtis!

Lilly
- has a yellow crown
- talks backwards
- eats cookie cutter-shaped sandwiches
- sleeps with ~~her crown~~

Wilson
- best friend is Chester

Chester
- best friend is Wilson
- rakes leaves
- double-knots his shoes
- uses hand signals when riding a bike

Chester's Way
Comparing and contrasting story characters, extending the story

"Chester and Wilson, Wilson and Chester. That's the way it was"…until Lilly moved into the neighborhood! After sharing the story with your class, encourage students to discuss how Chester, Wilson, and Lilly have their own unique ways of doing things. Then divide students into groups. Assign each group a different character: Chester, Wilson, or Lilly (some groups may have the same character). Instruct each group to write its character's name at the top of a sheet of tagboard. Next, have each group illustrate its assigned character on the tagboard beneath the name and then write characteristics about him or her around the illustration. After each group has shared its work, involve the students in a discussion of the similarities and differences among Chester, Wilson, and Lilly.

Culminate your lesson with the following activity. At the end of *Chester's Way*, Victor moves into the neighborhood. Challenge each student to write and illustrate another story about the four characters on a sheet of writing paper. Collect the pages and staple them between two construction paper covers; then add the title "The Many Adventures of Chester, Wilson, Lilly, *and* Victor" to the front cover. Place the completed book and a copy of *Chester's Way* in your reading center for all to enjoy!

Lilly's Purple Plastic Purse
Making a text-to-self connection

While out shopping with her grammy, Lilly receives glittery movie-star glasses and a purple plastic purse that plays music when you open it. And that's just the beginning of her new adventure! In advance, make several tagboard purse templates similar to the one shown. Read the story aloud as your students enjoy a snack of cheese balls—Lilly's favorite treat! Then challenge each youngster to write his own purple-purse adventure. To do this, the student traces a purse template onto a piece of white tagboard. He writes and illustrates a story on his purse; then he cuts the purse out. He covers the front of his cutout with purple plastic wrap and secures the wrap to the back of the purse with tape. Next, he punches two holes at the top of his purse as shown. To create a handle, he ties one end of a length of yarn through each of the holes. Provide time for youngsters to share their projects with their classmates.

Ryan

The day I got my purple purse, I went to the zoo. When I saw the monkeys, a monkey reached through the bars and tried to take it!
The End

Chrysanthemum

Writing poetry

Chrysanthemum loves her name; it is absolutely perfect—just like her. That is, until the kids at school start to tease her. After sharing the story, invite youngsters to discuss similar experiences they may have had with their own names. Then have each student create an acrostic poem about herself. To make an acrostic poem, a student writes her name vertically on a sheet of white paper; then she writes a phrase or word that begins with each letter in her name. She illustrates her poem as desired and glues it to a slightly larger sheet of construction paper. For added fun, collect the students' papers and read them aloud, one at a time, challenging the students to guess to whom each paper belongs. Youngsters will enjoy trying to match each student to her poem as they learn about their classmates.

Always polite
Likes cats
Eats pizza
Smiles a lot
Has a sister
Artistic

More Great Books by Kevin Henkes!

Clean Enough
Jessica
Julius, the Baby of the World
Sheila Rae, the Brave
A Weekend With Wendell

Mary Lester

Patterns

Use with *Good-bye, Curtis* on page 55.

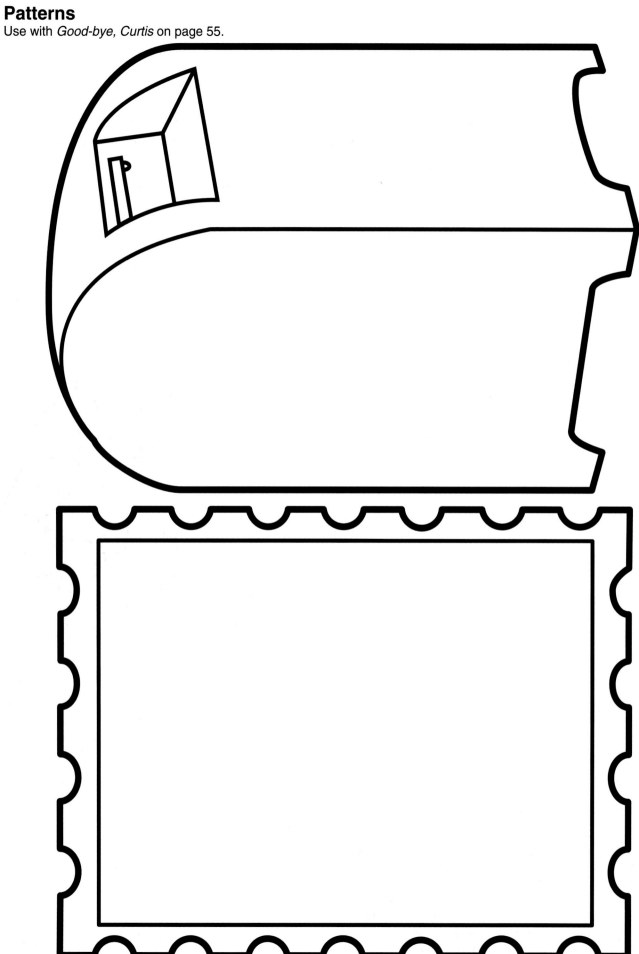

TIME FOR ICE CREAM!

Sweet and smooth, cold and creamy—ice cream is one of America's most popular dessert foods. Scoop up a gallon of learning fun with these ice-cream-related activities and ideas. They're "dairy" delightful!

ideas by Stacie Stone Davis

A Great Beginning
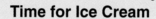
Participating in choral reading

Looking for a smooth way to introduce your unit on ice cream? Then teach your students the "Time for Ice Cream" rhyme about this dreamy, creamy dessert. Encourage students to create motions to accompany each verse.

Time for Ice Cream

Ice cream in the morning,
And in the afternoon.
Put some in a bowl,
And eat it with a spoon.

Ice cream in the evening.
Ice cream in the night.
Put some in a cone,
And eat every single bite!

Ice cream on the weekend,
And on a weekday, too.
Every day is ice-cream day.
I agree; do you?

I like to eat ice cream after I go swimming.

Any Time Is Ice-Cream Time 💻
Responding to a writing prompt

Any time might be ice-cream time, but students are bound to have a *favorite* time to eat it! In advance, glue a Styrofoam® ball on top of an ice-cream cone. To begin the activity, have each student use templates to trace a large cone shape onto brown construction paper and a large ice-cream-scoop shape onto a desired color of construction paper. Next, he glues the two shapes together to form an ice-cream cone. Then he uses a black marker to write "I like to eat ice cream [designated time]" on the paper cone. Take an instant photograph of each student holding the teacher-made ice-cream cone. To complete the project, have each student glue his snapshot on his ice-cream scoop. Mount the completed projects on a bulletin board titled "Time for Ice Cream!"

59

What's the Scoop?

Building on background knowledge

Share with students these fascinating facts about ice cream.

- The average American eats about 15 quarts of ice cream each year.
- No one knows for sure when ice cream was first made.
- The first ice-cream factory was built in 1851 by Baltimore milk dealer Jacob Fussell.
- Over ten percent of the milk produced in the United States is used in making ice cream.
- *Stabilizers* are used in making ice cream. They improve the ice cream's thickness and texture. Stabilizers are a mixture of *carrageenan,* which comes from a seaweed called Irish moss, and *guar gum,* which comes from a plant grown in India.

Cindy's Ice Cream
Flavor: Cocoaminty

Which Flavor Do You Favor?

Conducting a survey, organizing and interpreting data

No matter how you flavor it, ice cream is a favorite! About one-third of the ice cream sold in the United States is vanilla. Chocolate and Neapolitan rank next in popularity. But this information might not hold true in your school. Put your students to work surveying their schoolmates in an effort to determine the most popular ice-cream flavor at your school. To do this, arrange for each student (or student group) to visit a different classroom to survey the students about their favorite flavors of ice cream. Instruct each student (or a group recorder) to use tally marks to record the data. Back in the classroom, have the students compile the data on a graph. When the graph is complete, have students use the information to determine the most (or least) popular flavor of ice cream, and to create and solve a variety of word problems. Afterward, post the graph in a prominent school location so everyone can view the results. And the most popular flavor is…

Flavors of the Week

Collecting data, descriptive writing

What do Chunky Monkey®, Rocky Road, Wavy Gravy, Chubby Hubby®, and Rainforest Crunch™ have in common? As any good ice-cream aficionado knows, these are the names of ice-cream flavors. Encourage your students to uncover unusual ice-cream names the next time they visit the grocery store with their parents. Invite students to present their findings to their classmates. Record the different flavors on a large ice-cream-cone cutout.

Then, for a fun follow-up, challenge each student to create his own ice-cream flavor. Using the pattern on page 63, have each student name his ice-cream flavor, draw a picture of it, and describe the ingredients used in making it. Have the student cut out his ice-cream-pint pattern and glue it to a slightly larger sheet of colored construction paper. Compile the completed projects between two construction paper covers, add the title "Flavors of the Week," and place it at your reading center for everyone to sample. I'd like a double scoop of Cookie Dough Overload, please!

A Tasty Test
Using the senses to collect information

Challenge your young consumers to determine which brand of ice cream has the best flavor. To begin, tell students that differences in ice creams are a result of the quality, richness, and freshness of the ingredients used. Then have each student sample two different brands of vanilla ice cream—an off brand and a name brand—without revealing the identity of either brand. To do this, secretly label one brand of ice cream "A" and the other brand "B." First serve each student a sample of Brand A in a small cup; then repeat the procedure for Brand B. After students have tried both brands, ask them to vote to determine which brand they like best.

From Milk to Ice Cream
Recalling details from informational text, illustrating to show understanding

So how is ice cream made, anyway? Read aloud *From Cow to Ice Cream* by Bertram T. Knight to give students a better understanding of the process by which milk becomes ice cream. Afterward, enlist students' help in naming the main steps followed in the ice-cream-making process. Write each step on the bottom of a large sheet of construction paper. Then divide students into groups and give each group one of the labeled sheets. Using crayons or markers, each group illustrates the step printed on its paper. Bind the completed pages into a classroom book titled "From Milk to Ice Cream."

A Chilling Discovery
Comparing observations, drawing a logical conclusion

Students will be surprised to learn that milk, ice, sugar, *and* salt are the ingredients for homemade ice-cream recipes. But students are sure to realize that salt doesn't belong *in* the ice-cream mixture! Explain to students the role of salt in this experiment. Place ten ice cubes in each of two clean, 16-ounce metal cans. Label one can "salt"; then stir seven tablespoons of salt into that can. Leave both cans to sit undisturbed for about five minutes. Afterward, have students examine the cans and compare their observations. The outside of the ice-filled can has *condensation,* or a buildup of water. The can containing the ice and the salt has a frosty exterior. Tell students that the salt lowers the temperature of the ice in the can, causing the condensation on the outside of the can to freeze. Then ask students to explain why a container of ice-cream mixture might be placed inside a salty ice mixture. Lead students to understand that the salt creates a colder temperature at which the ice-cream mix can freeze.

Clevell Harris

61

The Ice-Cream Parlor 💻
Solving math facts

Create an ice-cream parlor with this "scooper-duper" center that tempts your students to practice their math facts. Decorate a corner of your classroom with an ice-cream-parlor backdrop. Cover a table with a plastic tablecloth. Place plastic milk shake glasses and straws on the table. Collect some menus from a local ice-cream shoppe and place them on the table.

Next, cut out several banana-split dish, banana, and ice-cream-scoop shapes from construction paper. Glue each banana to a banana-split dish as shown. Place three scoop cutouts with each resulting dish. Program each dish with a different math sum compatible with your students' abilities. Next, program each of the three scoops for each dish with a different math fact that equals the sum on its corresponding dish. Write the answers on the backs for self-checking. Laminate all the pieces for durability. Store the pieces in a clean ice-cream container at the center. A student visits the ice-cream parlor, removes the cutouts from the container, and matches the scoops to the correct dishes. She then flips the scoops to check her work. Mmmm, delicious!

The Real Thing, Please!
Using appropriate tools to measure capacity, following directions

No doubt by now your youngsters have a hankering for some ice cream. So top off your unit with this easy-to-make recipe for ice cream. Pair students and invite each pair to make its own ice cream. If desired, ask parents to send in additional ice-cream flavors and toppings—such as chocolate syrup, sprinkles, and nuts—for students to use in creating tantalizing ice-cream treats. Be prepared—students will be "ice-screaming" for more!

Ice Cream in a Can

Each student pair will need:

1 bowl
1 small metal can
crushed ice
rock salt
1 spoon
1/2 c. milk
1/2 c. half-and-half
1/4 c. sugar
1/4 tsp. vanilla

Combine the half-and-half, milk, sugar, and vanilla in the can. Place the can in the middle of the bowl; then pack ice and rock salt around the can. Stir the mixture for five minutes. Next, cover the can's opening with plastic wrap and set it aside (still in the bowl) for approximately 30 minutes. If the ice cream is still soft, place the can in the freezer until the ice cream hardens.

_____'s Ice Cream
(student)

Flavor: _____

Draw a picture of your ice cream.

Description: _____

_____

_____

_____

One pint

Take your students on an imaginary safari through Africa. There they'll meet enormous elephants, leaping leopards, and a host of other world-famous African animals. So what are you waiting for? Pack your bags and grab your passports!

ideas by Cynthia Holcomb

HEADING ON A SAFARI!

Building background knowledge, following directions

An African safari used to be a hunting trip, but now it is an organized trip to view and photograph the intriguing wild animals that live in Africa. Most safaris last 10 to 21 days and participants often travel in jeeps. Introduce your youngsters to this fascinating experience by reading aloud *Jungle Jack Hanna's Safari Adventure* by Jack Hanna and Rick A. Prebeg. Captivating photos and informative text deliver an inside look at a zoologist's safari through East Africa. After reading the book aloud, have students make jeep journals before they embark on their safari. To make a journal, a student cuts out a white construction paper copy of the jeep pattern on page 74. Next, he uses the cutout as a template to trace and cut out a desired number of journal-writing pages and a construction paper back cover. To complete the journal, he staples the writing pages between the two covers, draws a picture of himself in the driver's seat, and personalizes the remainder of the cover as desired. Then, throughout the expedition, ask students to note interesting animal facts in their journals. Beep! Beep! Get ready—your safari is now under way!

HOME, SWEET HOME

Connecting animals to their environments, using map skills

What kinds of animals can you find in Africa? It depends on the area you explore. Using the reproducible map on page 75, lead students to realize that a variety of animals are found in Africa—not just the ever popular elephants, giraffes, and lions. Introduce the color code; then lead students around the continent. As students color their maps, share the following facts about Africa's three main types of environments:

- The wettest region in Africa is the rain forest, where it rains almost every day. Approximately one-fifth of Africa is rain forest and home to such animals as gorillas, chimpanzees, monkeys, wild pigs, hippopotamuses, and snakes. You will also find a bevy of birds, such as flamingos, pelicans, herons, storks, and kingfishers.

- The desert region is a much drier climate. About two-fifths of Africa is desert, and the animals that live there must survive the dry conditions. The desert is home to camels, foxes, jackals, boars, hyenas, and gazelles.

- The *savanna* (or grassland) region is a flat, grassy area where few trees grow. More than two-fifths of the continent is covered with these grasslands. Most of the larger animals of Africa—such as elephants, rhinoceroses, wildebeests, giraffes, zebras, and buffaloes—live in the savanna. It is also home to the big cats—lions, cheetahs, and leopards—and to a big bird, the ostrich.

To complete the activity, have each student cut out the animals and use the map key to glue the cutouts to their corresponding regions (either square for the region is correct). At the completion of this activity, students will feel as if they've already had a firsthand tour of the continent!

WHAT ANIMALS LIVE IN AFRICA? 🖥

Building background knowledge

Share these interesting facts about some of Africa's most celebrated animals with your students:

- The *elephant,* the largest land animal, has larger ears than any other animal, and its tusks are the largest teeth. This animal usually eats about 300 pounds of vegetation a day.
- The *giraffe,* with its long neck, is the tallest of all animals. Its unique coat has yellowish brown patchlike markings that make it hard to see when it stands among trees.
- There are three types of *zebras* in Africa, each with a distinctive stripe pattern. The stripes help to keep herds of zebras together. In addition, no two zebras have identical stripes.
- The *lion* spends about 20 hours a day sleeping or resting. It lives in a group of typically 10 to 20 lions called a *pride.* It prefers to eat large prey such as zebra, antelope, and buffalo.
- The *ostrich,* the largest of all birds, has two toes on each foot (the longest toe being seven inches long). It cannot fly, but it can run very fast. The male ostrich makes a roar-hiss sound.
- Two species of *rhinoceros* live in Africa—the white and the black. The white rhino is actually gray and the black rhino is a darker gray. Each has two horns that grow from its nose throughout its life.
- The *antelope,* with its hollow horns, belongs to the same animal family as goats. The most common type of antelope has a smooth coat of brown or gray hair.
- The *leopard,* with its tan fur and black spots, lives both on the ground and in trees. On the ground, this large cat blends in with its surroundings.
- The *hippopotamus* can swim underwater—with its nose and ears closed—for up to six minutes.
- The *buffalo,* a type of large black ox that lives in Africa, is known to have a bad temper and can be dangerous.

SAFARI CHATTER

Set the stage for lots of safari antics by inviting your students to choose African animal names for team and small-group activities. Suggest names like Exceptional Elephants, Awesome Antelopes, Zany Zebras, and Outstanding Ostriches; then invite students to brainstorm additional names. The thematic names could also be assigned to rows or groups of student desks: "The Great Giraffes may line up for lunch!"

WHAT'S IN A NAME?

Exploring the origin of animal names

Rhinoceros, hippopotamus, elephant—these names can be quite a mouthful! Have your students investigate animal names with this unique activity. Write each of the following animal names on a sheet of bulletin board paper. Also write the meaning of each word on a separate sentence strip. Mount the chart in a prominent location. Then have student volunteers match each meaning to its corresponding name. If desired, tell students the language of each name's origin. For an added challenge, have students create meanings for other animals, such as the elephant, lion, monkey, and parrot. Provide time for students to share their meanings with their classmates.

Animal Name	Original Meaning	Origin of Name
alligator	the lizard	Spanish
camel	carrying a burden	Middle Eastern
giraffe	one that walks very fast	Arabic
gorilla	hairy person	African
hippopotamus	river horse	Greek
rhinoceros	horn on the nose	Greek

ANIMAL GROUPS

Investigating animal behavior, building vocabulary

What's more fun than a band of monkeys? How about a herd of elephants! Explain to students that some animals live together in groups. In many groups, the adults will work together to defend their young from an attacking animal. Some groups, such as herds of elephants, remain together for many years. Share with students the provided list of animal group names; then have students use the information to create murals of African animal groups. To begin, divide students into eight groups and assign each group an animal from the chart. Have each group draw several illustrations of its animal on a sheet of bulletin board paper. Then have the group label the resulting animal group with its name from the chart. Mount the murals in the hallway to create a swingin' safari!

Animal	Group
camel	herd
elephant	herd
giraffe	herd
lion	pride
monkey	band/troop
ostrich	flock
zebra	herd
hippopotamus	pod

A herd of zebras

MONKEYING AROUND!

Recalling facts from informational text, comparing animal characteristics

What do apes, monkeys, and human beings have in common? They are all *primates.* Primates do not have hooves or paws; they have hands and feet that can grasp and hold. Monkeys, as well as two members of the ape family (gorillas and chimpanzees), live in Africa. Apes are different from monkeys in the following ways:

- Monkeys have tails. They use their tails to balance and grip as they run along tree branches.
- Apes have longer arms than legs. They use their arms to take their weight as they walk. Their arms also help them swing (rather than run) through the trees.

To provide students with additional information about monkeys and apes, read aloud *Monkeys, Apes, and Other Primates* translated by Vicki Bogard. With information designed especially for the young learner, this nonfiction book tells about the biggest, the smallest, the strongest, the most clever, and all the other primates in between. At the conclusion of the book, have each student write a fact from the book on a banana-shaped cutout. Then staple the completed cutouts to a bulletin board titled "We Know a Whole Bunch About Primates!"

All apes live in the forest.

Apes eat fruit, leaves, and insects.

Monkeys run along branches on all fours.

ELEPHANT STORIES

Investigating an animal appendage, creative writing

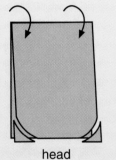
head

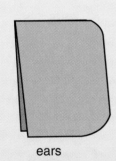
ears

Katelyn

Everything about elephants is big—especially their trunks. With over 60,000 muscles, an elephant's trunk can do a variety of things. Besides breathing and smelling, it's also used for drinking, picking up food, digging, showering, snorkeling, trumpeting, and spraying on dust to stop sunburn and insect bites. After sharing this information with students, have each child write a story starring an elephant on a 5 1/2" x 8" sheet of paper. Suggest writing topics such as "The Elephant Who Lost His Trunk," "Ten New Uses for an Elephant's Trunk," and "How to Take Care of an Elephant Who Has a Cold."

Have students staple their completed stories in between elephant-shaped journals. To make a journal, a student folds a 6" x 18" piece of gray construction paper in half. Holding the fold at the top, she rounds the bottom corners of the front cover. To create ears, she folds in half another 6" x 18" piece of gray construction paper, trims the corners as shown, unfolds the paper, and cuts on the fold line. She then glues the resulting ears to the back cover. To create a trunk, she glues a 3" x 18" gray construction paper strip under the bottom edge of the front cover. She writes her name vertically on the strip and then uses a pencil to roll the strip under so that it curls. Next, she adds facial features using construction paper scraps, markers, or crayons. Finally, she staples her elephant story between the covers. Display the completed projects on a classroom wall titled "Trumpeting Great Stories!"

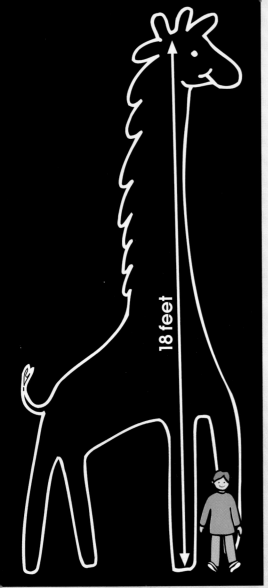

18 feet

SIZING UP GIRAFFES

Measuring length using standard and nonstandard units, making comparisons

The giraffe, the tallest living animal, can grow to 18 feet in height. Its legs alone are about six feet long, its neck can be from six to eight feet long, and its tongue is 18 inches long. Use this activity to help your students discover how they measure up to giraffes. To begin, have student volunteers use chalk and yardsticks to draw a line 18 feet long on an outdoor blacktop surface. As students evaluate the line, explain that it represents how tall the giraffe would be if it were lying down. Next, as students sit on the line, complete a chalk outline of a giraffe around them. Then have each student, in turn, lie down beside the drawing while you mark her height compared to the giraffe. For added fun see how many students it takes, lying head to toe, to equal the giraffe's height. Wow! Giraffes are tall!

YIKES! STRIPES!

Investigating animal defenses, understanding the role of the outer ear in hearing

As you enter the grassy plains of Africa, watch out for speeding stripes! Zebras are peaceful animals, often grazing with antelopes and ostriches, but they can reach speeds of 40 mph when stalked by an enemy such as a lion, hyena, or cheetah. Zebras protect themselves from predators by keeping together in a herd. They also have large ears that rotate to locate sounds indicating an enemy is nearby.

To help students understand the benefit of a zebra's rotating ears, have students cup their hands behind their ears. Next, have them turn around so that their backs are to you. Announce a desired sentence to students. Then, with their ears still cupped, have students turn in the direction of the sound. Repeat the same sentence. Ask students to determine which way they can hear more clearly—with their ears away from the sound or facing it. No doubt students will be all ears for this demonstration!

HANDSOME ANIMAL MASKS

Using assorted art media to communicate an idea

These handsome masks are perfect for complementing your study of African animals. For each student cut an eyehole window from a paper plate. Have each student use a variety of art supplies—such as pom-poms, pipe cleaners, feathers, markers, yarn, and construction paper scraps—to create a mask portraying a desired African animal. After students complete their masks, tape a paint-stirring stick to the back of each mask. Then invite each youngster to model his mask and tell about the animal it represents.

INTERVIEW THE ANIMALS

Researching animals, exploring point of view through writing

Encourage your students to learn about Africa's many animals from an up-close and personal point of view. Ask each student to select an African animal to research. Provide reference materials for each student to use as she completes a copy of the interview form on page 76. Instruct her to answer the questions on the reproducible from her animal's point of view. After students have completed the questions, ask each student, in turn, to present her information. To do this, she takes a seat in the front of the classroom. Ask her a question from the reproducible and, without revealing the animal, have her answer as her animal would. At the end of her presentation, have her call on her classmates to identify her animal. The student who guesses correctly becomes the next presenter. Your students are sure to enjoy the chance to be safari sleuths!

ANIMAL-CRACKER FUN

Using manipulatives for skill reinforcement

Students will be hungry for more fun when they complete these hands-on activities. Empty the contents of at least five boxes of animal crackers into a bowl, discarding the crackers that are not African animals. Place the crackers, a supply of drawing paper, glue, pencils, and crayons at a center.

- To provide practice patterning, have each student use the crackers to create a variety of patterns. If desired, have students record their patterns on drawing paper.
- For estimation fun, place the animal crackers in a clear container. Have each student record his estimate of the number of crackers. Then, as a class, count to find the answer.
- Have students use the animal crackers to figure addition, subtraction, or multiplication problems. Write the problems on numbered index cards and have students record their answers on paper if desired.
- Have each student glue a desired animal cracker to a sheet of paper and then write a poem or story about the animal. (Be sure to place extra crackers at the center for this activity.)
- To provide practice with alphabetical order, glue different African animal crackers on separate index cards. Label the animals; then place the cards at the center. Have each student place the animal cards in alphabetical order and record his answers on the provided paper.

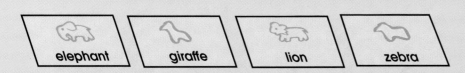

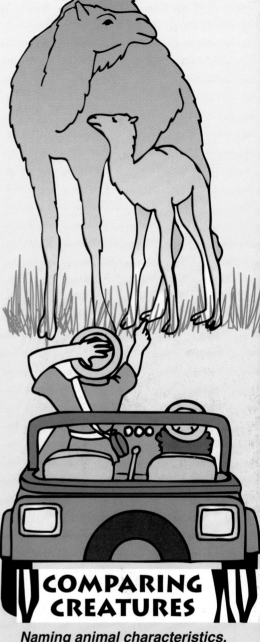

COMPARING CREATURES

Naming animal characteristics, organizing information on a diagram

This partner activity is just the ticket for exploring the similarities and differences between African animals. To begin, pair students and have each partner choose a different African animal. Have each student list five to eight characteristics of his animal on a sheet of scrap paper and then share the list with his partner. Next, have the partners refer to their lists as they complete a copy of the reproducible on page 77. Conclude this activity by having the student pairs share the common characteristics of their animals with their classmates.

69

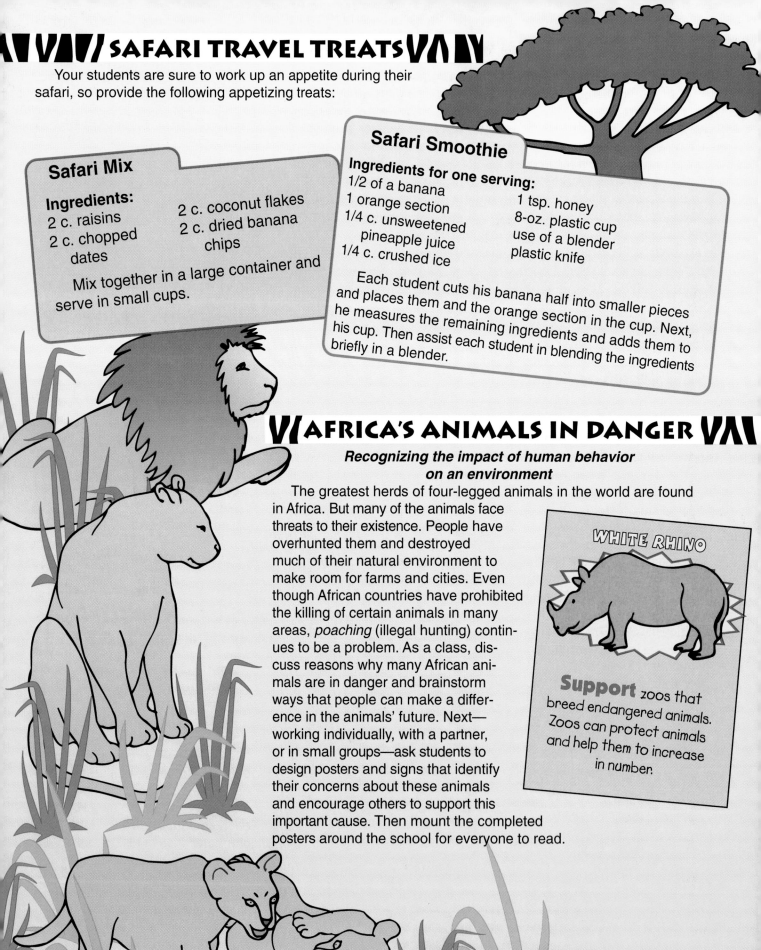

SAFARI TRAVEL TREATS

Your students are sure to work up an appetite during their safari, so provide the following appetizing treats:

Safari Mix

Ingredients:
2 c. raisins
2 c. chopped dates
2 c. coconut flakes
2 c. dried banana chips

Mix together in a large container and serve in small cups.

Safari Smoothie

Ingredients for one serving:
1/2 of a banana
1 orange section
1/4 c. unsweetened pineapple juice
1/4 c. crushed ice
1 tsp. honey
8-oz. plastic cup
use of a blender
plastic knife

Each student cuts his banana half into smaller pieces and places them and the orange section in the cup. Next, he measures the remaining ingredients and adds them to his cup. Then assist each student in blending the ingredients briefly in a blender.

AFRICA'S ANIMALS IN DANGER

Recognizing the impact of human behavior on an environment

The greatest herds of four-legged animals in the world are found in Africa. But many of the animals face threats to their existence. People have overhunted them and destroyed much of their natural environment to make room for farms and cities. Even though African countries have prohibited the killing of certain animals in many areas, *poaching* (illegal hunting) continues to be a problem. As a class, discuss reasons why many African animals are in danger and brainstorm ways that people can make a difference in the animals' future. Next—working individually, with a partner, or in small groups—ask students to design posters and signs that identify their concerns about these animals and encourage others to support this important cause. Then mount the completed posters around the school for everyone to read.

WHITE RHINO

Support zoos that breed endangered animals. Zoos can protect animals and help them to increase in number.

⚁ POSTCARDS FROM THE SAFARI ⚁

Writing and addressing a postcard

No trip is ever complete without a chance to write postcards—and a safari is no exception! Provide each student with an index card. Have each youngster illustrate one side of his card with a favorite African animal. Then, on the back of his card, ask him to write a brief, informative caption about his illustration in the upper left-hand corner. Next, have him write a message to a family member or friend in which he tells about his safari trip. Help the students address their resulting postcards before affixing animal stickers for postage. The recipients of these hand-delivered postcards are sure to feel extraspecial indeed!

An adult male gorilla can be six feet tall when standing.

Dear Mom and Dad,
    I had a great time on our safari. I learned all about African animals. The gorilla is my favorite because it is a primate like me.
        Love,
        Joseph

Mom & Dad Murphy
1234 Lenoir Dr.
Greensboro, NC 27410

⚁ SAFARI SOUVENIRS ⚁

Using nonstandard art media

Culminate your safari with these keepsake pins. Give each student an animal cracker in the shape of an African animal. Then have each student use acrylic paints to paint the front of her cracker as desired. Allow the paint to dry; then apply a clear acrylic sealer to each cracker. Finally, use a hot glue gun to attach a bar pin to the back of each cracker. Encourage students to wear their pins as a remembrance of the amazing animals of Africa.

71

A LITERARY SAFARI

Don't leave the continent without visiting these African animal books.

RAYMOND FLOYD GOES TO AFRICA, OR THERE ARE NO BEARS IN AFRICA

by Cynthia H. Murdock

Making a personal connection

Students may be taking a tour of African wildlife, but one thing they won't find is a bear! That is, unless you share this delightful story with your students. Raymond Floyd, a stuffed bear less than two inches tall, journeys through Africa while riding on the hat of his friend Mrs. Moose. Raymond meets zebras, elephants, lions, and a host of other African animals during his travels. Your students will enjoy making the acquaintance of each animal as Raymond introduces himself to creatures around the continent. After sharing the story, have each student draw a picture of herself meeting one of the animals from the story. Encourage students to write what they would say to the animals in speech bubbles. Display the completed projects on a bulletin board titled "Take an African Wildlife Tour!"

JUMANJI

by Chris Van Allsburg

Responding to literature, working cooperatively toward a common goal

What would it be like to have African animals come for a visit? It wouldn't be all fun and games, as your students will find out. In this story, two restless youngsters find a board game and play it without reading all the directions. Little do they know that each square they land on will bring adventurous results—right into their living room! After reading the story aloud, pair students and challenge each pair to design a safari board game. Supply each student pair with a manila file folder, a supply of markers, and a die. Challenge the students to create board games similar to the one in the story. Encourage them to include African animals in the directions for each square on their gameboards. Provide time for each pair to present its completed game to the class. Then store the games in a convenient location for students to play during free time. Anyone up for a little adventure?

MORE FICTIONAL FAVORITES ABOUT AFRICAN ANIMALS

Dr. De Soto Goes to Africa
by William Steig

Africa Calling: Nighttime Falling
by Daniel Adlerman

How Snake Got His Hiss: An Original Tale
by Marguerite W. Davol

The Lonely Lioness and the Ostrich Chicks: A Masai Tale
retold by Verna Aardema

Why Mosquitoes Buzz in People's Ears: A West African Tale
by Verna Aardema

Bringing the Rain to Kapiti Plain
by Verna Aardema

Zella, Zack, and Zodiac
by Bill Peet

SILVERSTEIN SAFARI

Not packed with facts but full of fun are Shel Silverstein's books about African animals. Your students will enjoy the humor in the following playful stories:

A Giraffe and a Half
Told in couplets, this rollicking rhyme will have students wanting a giraffe of their own.

Who Wants a Cheap Rhinoceros?
Have you ever considered having a pet rhino? This story will advise you on what fun it might be!

A NONFICTION FAVORITE

African Animals by Caroline Arnold features superb full-color photographs of almost two dozen African species in their habitats.

Pattern
Use with "Heading on a Safari!" on page 64.

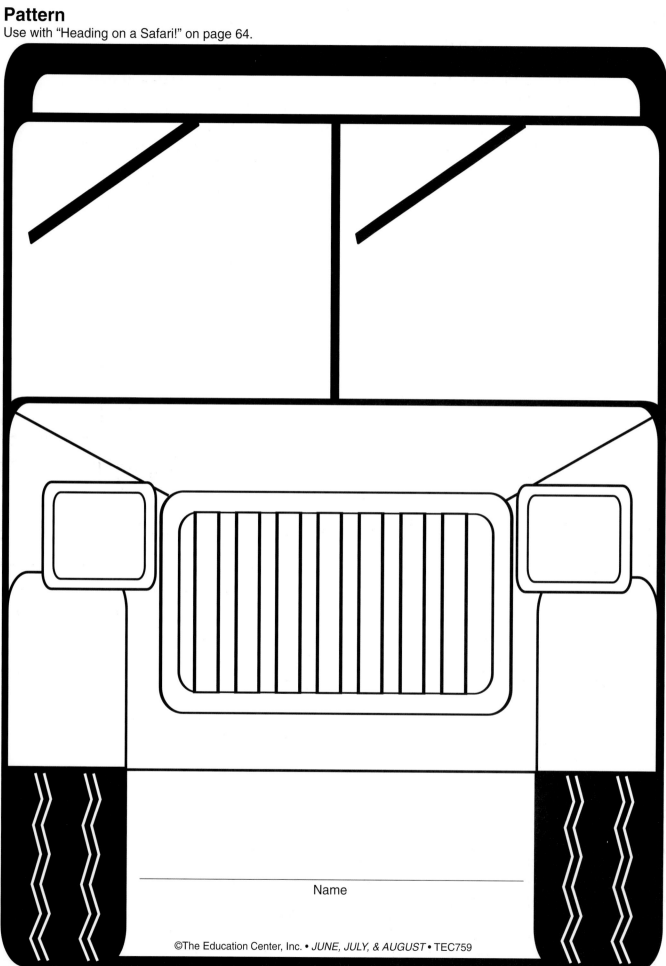

Name

ALL AROUND AFRICA

Use the code to color the map.
Cut out the animals.
Use the map key to glue each animal to a square
  pointing to its home.

Color Code

desert = brown

rain forest = green

savanna = yellow

Map Key

camel	
rhino	
fennec fox	
chimp	
ostrich	
gorilla	

©The Education Center, Inc. • *JUNE, JULY, & AUGUST* • TEC759

fennec fox   **chimp**   **camel**   **ostrich**   **gorilla**   **rhino**

Note to the teacher: Use with "Home, Sweet Home" on page 64.

AFRICAN ANIMAL INTERVIEW

Choose an animal to research.
Pretend you are the animal.
Answer each question.

1. What is your habitat (or place you live) like?

   _____

   _____

2. What do you like to eat?

   _____

   _____

3. How tall are you? _____

4. How much do you weigh? _____

5. What color are you? _____

6. How do you protect yourself?

   _____

   _____

7. What are two interesting facts about yourself?

   _____

   _____

8. What animal are you? _____

Name _____

CREATURE COMPARISONS

Write words that describe Animal One on the left.
Write words that describe Animal Two on the right.
Write words that describe both animals on the tree.

Both

Animal One: _____

Animal Two: _____

©The Education Center, Inc. • *JUNE, JULY, & AUGUST* • TEC759

77 **Note to the teacher:** Use with "Comparing Creatures" on page 69.

Count On Me!
Math Activities to Start the Year

These getting-acquainted activities add up to loads of fun! Introduce your students to everyday math matters and learn more about your class in the bargain. Students will use dozens of math skills to learn about themselves and their classmates. Now that's "sum" way to launch a school year!

ideas by Amy Erickson and Nicole Iacovazzi

Sort and Tell
Identifying attributes used for sorting

Students will have all sorts of fun classifying their favorite stuffed animals in this activity! Ask each student to bring one of his favorite stuffed animals to school on a predetermined day. Be sure to have a few extra stuffed animals available for students who don't bring one. Once everyone has an animal, direct students to place their animals in a designated area of the classroom. Have a student volunteer sort the animals and ask his classmates to guess how he grouped them. Did he sort by size? Outfits? Type of fur? After several students have guessed, ask the volunteer to tell his rule for sorting. Select additional volunteers to take turns sorting the animals into different groups and challenging their classmates to guess the categories. This classified information will surely capture your students' interest!

Three students have only cats.

The number of students who have only dogs is the same.

More girls than boys have only dogs.

Sets of Pets
Organizing information on a diagram, explaining results in writing

Millions of Cats by Wanda Ga'g is the "purr-fect cat-alyst" for a math activity on collecting data. This endearing book tells about a lonely couple who think having a pet cat would brighten their lives. After sharing the book, lead students in a discussion about the pets they own. Draw a large Venn diagram on the chalkboard, and label one side "cats," the other side "dogs," and the middle section "both." Ask each student to write her name in the appropriate section. When all of the data has been gathered, have students analyze the diagram to determine how many students have dogs, cats, dogs and cats, and neither dogs nor cats. Then, to assess students' understanding of the information, have each student write sentences about her interpretation of the information. No doubt this activity will be the cat's meow!

Shapely Names
Using visualization and spatial reasoning

Reasoning is the name of this math game! Students will put their problem-solving skills to the test when they try to match name shapes with the corresponding people. Lightly writing one letter per square, have each student write his first name on the top line of one-inch graph paper. Ask him to continue by writing his middle name, if any, on the second line. Then have him write his last name on the next line in a similar fashion. Instruct students to conceal their writing by using a crayon to carefully color each block that has a letter. Then have them cut out the resulting colored shapes. Post the shapes on a bulletin board titled "Guess Who!" Challenge students to identify who made each figure. Students will be eager to see how their guesswork scores!

Phone Fun
Estimating sums beyond basic facts

This activity adds up to a "phon-omenally" good time! Students will familiarize themselves with several useful telephone numbers and call on a variety of math skills as they create personalized telephone directories. In advance, gather a few telephone books for students to use as needed. To create a directory for each student, stack three sheets of duplicating paper, fold the paper in half, and staple on the fold. Invite students to personalize the resulting covers with crayons. On the first page of his directory, have the student write his telephone number. Next, have him collect the telephone numbers of nine different classmates, businesses, or emergency services and record and label each phone number on either the front or back of a separate page of his directory. After students have recorded the numbers, explain that they will be adding the digits in each of them. Have each student predict which of the ten telephone numbers will have the greatest sum and which will have the smallest. Then have him add to determine the actual totals and record each sum on its corresponding page. (If desired, provide calculators for this task.) Engage students in a discussion about their results. They're sure to talk about this activity for a long time to come!

"Feet-uring" Remarkable Rulers
Using nonstandard units to estimate and measure length

Step right up to this idea that reinforces measurement skills! Explain to students that each of them will be measuring with a nonstandard unit: her foot. To begin, have each student trace her foot onto a sheet of construction paper and cut out the resulting shape. Instruct each child to estimate the number of foot cutouts equal to her height and to record and label her estimate on her foot cutout. Then pair students and ask each child to help her partner use her cutout to determine her actual height. Have her record it below her estimate.

Next, have students brainstorm a list of other things that they could measure with their foot cutouts, such as the widths of their desks, the length of the chalkboard, the perimeter of the classroom, and the distance from the classroom to the water fountain. Then have each student estimate and measure several items from the list. Remind students to record their work on their foot cutouts. For an added challenge, have students measure their cutouts with rulers and then convert the previously recorded measurements to standard units. Students will undoubtedly enjoy putting their best feet forward as they work!

It's Time!
Showing an understanding of telling time, expository writing

Your class will be up-to-the-minute with this approach to teaching the concept of time. Distribute copies of the reproducible on page 84. At five different times during the day, spontaneously declare, "It's time!" Have each child stop what she is doing, draw hands for the actual time on a clock face, and write the corresponding time below the clock. Then direct her to write the activity in which she is engaged on the lines adjacent to the clock. Be sure you make note of the times as well. At the end of the day, announce the times that should be listed on students' papers and invite students to share the corresponding activities. For an added challenge, have each student take home an extra copy of the reproducible to record five weekend activities in a similar fashion. In no time at all, your students will gain a better understanding of how quickly time flies!

Math on a Budget

Showing number sense, adding money amounts

Cash in on this "toy-riffic" idea for some real-life shopping excitement! Have students brainstorm birthday gifts that they would like to receive. Write their responses on the chalkboard. Choose a few items from the list and ask students to estimate their prices. Write their estimates on the board. Then have students use a variety of catalogs and sales circulars to determine the actual prices of the selected items.

Next, send your students on a birthday buying spree. To begin, tell students that they will each have an imaginary budget of $100 to "purchase" birthday gifts. Each student writes his birthday list on a sheet of paper. Then he searches through toy catalogs and sales circulars to find the prices of his items and records them on his list. Next, he adds the prices of his gifts to determine their total cost and modifies his list as needed to stay within his $100 budget. Once he has finalized his list, he records each item and its price on a separate 5 1/2" x 8 1/2" sheet of duplicating paper; then he illustrates each gift. After he has recorded and illustrated all of the items, he uses crayons and a gift bow to personalize and decorate one 6" x 9" sheet of construction paper to resemble a gift box. Then he stacks the construction paper atop the other pages and staples the pages. What a profitable way to learn about your students' interests and provide practice with adding money as well!

Nick Greenwood

Math That's Totally Me 💻

Using manipulatives to represent equivalent forms of the same number

This math center adds up to lots of birthday fun! Store a supply of two different colors of birthday candles and a cake cutout in a birthday gift bag. Place the bag, crayons, and a supply of blank paper at a center. A student removes the cake cutout and the candles from the bag. She then uses the cutout and candles to determine number combinations that total her age. For example, four green candles and two yellow ones on a cake could depict six years. Three green candles and three yellow ones is another possibility. After determining each number combination, she sketches a likeness of the birthday cake and writes and solves the corresponding addition problem as shown on her paper. The student continues in this manner until she has determined all the possible addition combinations for her age.

After everyone has completed this center, group students who are the same age and ask them to compare the different combinations that they discovered. Then lead students in a discussion about the individual strategies they used to complete the activity and any patterns they noticed. It won't be long before your students are old hands at working with numbers!

Closet Confusion
Using the make-a-list strategy

Dress your students for success with this problem-solving activity! Ask students if they ever have difficulty deciding what to wear. Then announce that they are going to determine how many different outfits are possible with just two shirts, two pairs of pants, and two pairs of shoes.

Duplicate page 85 onto white construction paper for each student. Have each student personalize, color, and cut out the figure and clothing on his copy. Challenge each child to find eight different outfits. Have the students use the numerals on the pieces of clothing to record the different combinations on their papers. After each student has discovered all possible outfits, ask him to glue one of the outfits on the figure to resemble himself. Provide an opportunity at the end of this session for students to share their strategies for solving the problem and their results. Students will love tackling math in style!

Window on My Week 🖥
Making and dating a daily entry to show passage of time

Schedule some time to bring your students' calendar skills up-to-date. To begin, share the delightful book *Cookie's Week* by Cindy Ward. This humorous story summarizes one cat's eventful week. After reading the book aloud, have each student create her own weekly log. To make a log, each child stacks nine sheets of 8 1/2" x 5 1/2" duplicating paper and staples them together on the left side. She then titles the resulting book "Window on My Week," writes an appropriate byline, and draws a window on her cover.

Have each student complete a page in her log each day. To do this, have her write the day, date, and something that happened that day. Encourage all students to illustrate their text. Have students conclude their books with a page titled "About the Author." Students' chronicles of the week will surely become keepsakes that they will read time and again!

Window on My Week by Ann

On Tuesday, Sept. 2, I went to the park.

Math-Related Literature

One Hundred Is a Family

by Pam Muñoz Ryan
Developing number sense

Explore the many meanings of *family* with this beautifully illustrated picture book. Its rhyming text lists some of the many types of families to which people belong. For example, "SIXTY is a family sharing a neighborhood street," and "SEVENTY is a family fixing a festive place to meet." Challenge your class to generate a new version of this story, beginning with one and continuing as high as possible. To do this, gather your students in a circle. Start the activity by stating and completing the following sentence starter: "One is a family…" Choose a student in the circle to continue with two. Proceed clockwise around the circle in the same fashion until the class is stumped. Students' understanding of family will surely be enhanced, and their proficiency with number concepts will increase as well!

My Little Sister Ate One Hare

by Bill Grossman
Using place value to organize data

No doubt your students are always eager to recount the trials of having siblings. This entertaining book is a forum for one boy to do just that. In this outrageous cumulative tale a boy details the unbelievable meal his younger sister eats. Her menu includes lizards with their heads and legs and gizzards, and worms with all their germs. Before reading the book aloud, survey your students to determine how many brothers and sisters each of them has. To do so, ask each student to take one blue Unifix® cube for each brother he has and one green cube for each sister. Then, as a class, use the blue cubes to construct towers in sets of ten. Repeat the procedure with the green cubes. Ask the students to count the cubes by tens and analyze the towers. Do students have more brothers or sisters? How many more?

Next, read the book aloud and have students guess the total number of things that the little sister eats. Invite students to share their guesses; then have students record the numbers on a sheet of paper as you reread the book. It's for certain: this math activity about siblings rivals all others!

A House Is a House for Me 💻

by Mary Ann Hoberman
Recognizing real-world application of numbers

This delightful story, told in verse, is packed with clever references to a variety of things and each of their dwellings. After sharing the story, have each child use a template to trace and cut out two house shapes from white construction paper. Then have him align his shapes and staple them at the top. Have each student personalize the top shape of his resulting booklet to resemble his own home. Then have students brainstorm the roles that numbers play for them at home, such as apartment or house numbers, numbers of rooms, numbers of windows, telephone numbers, and numbers of siblings. Instruct students to record these and other number-related facts on the second page of their booklets. Display the completed projects on a bulletin board to create a nifty neighborhood of numbers.

It's Time!

11 12 1 / 10 · 2 / 9 · 3 / 8 · 4 / 7 6 5 / ____ : ____	_____ _____ _____
11 12 1 / 10 · 2 / 9 · 3 / 8 · 4 / 7 6 5 / ____ : ____	_____ _____ _____
11 12 1 / 10 · 2 / 9 · 3 / 8 · 4 / 7 6 5 / ____ : ____	_____ _____ _____
11 12 1 / 10 · 2 / 9 · 3 / 8 · 4 / 7 6 5 / ____ : ____	_____ _____ _____
11 12 1 / 10 · 2 / 9 · 3 / 8 · 4 / 7 6 5 / ____ : ____	_____ _____ _____

Note to the teacher: Use this reproducible with "It's Time!" on page 80.

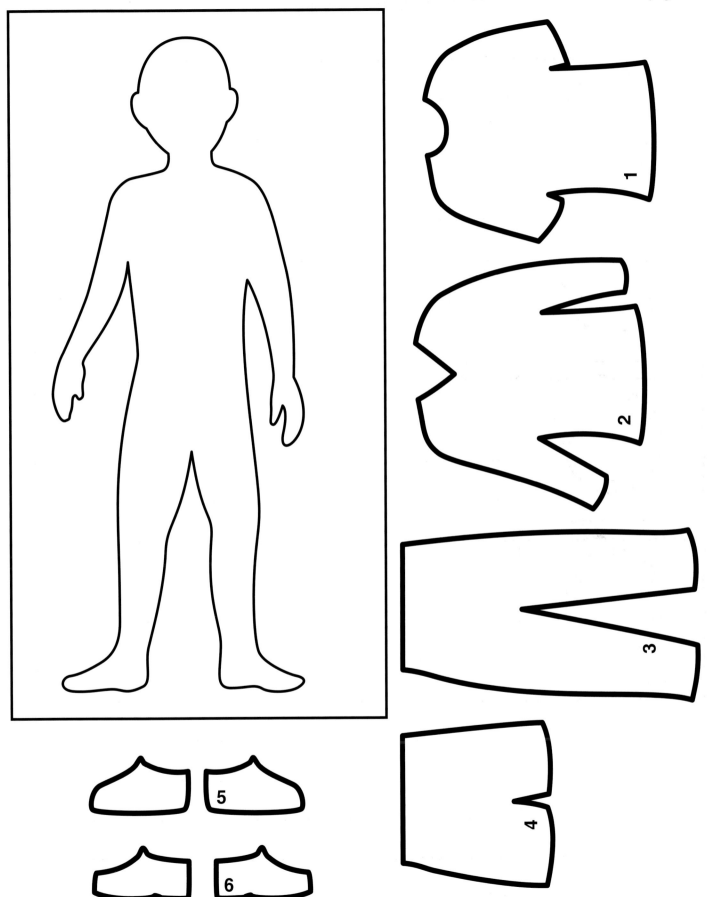

The Sky's the Limit!

High-Flying Activities for Teaching Flight and Aviation

Fasten your seat belts and investigate the world of flight and aviation with this collection of creative activities. Whether you use these ideas to celebrate National Aviation Day on August 19 or add them to your science lesson plans, excitement is sure to soar as students explore the wild blue yonder! Happy landing!

ideas by Lisa Buchholz, Brenda McGee, and Susan Hohbach Walker

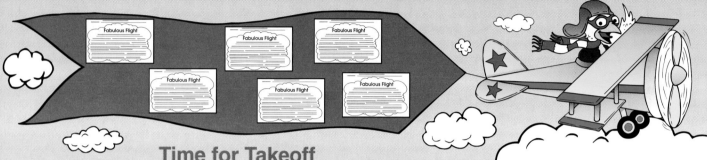

Time for Takeoff

Recalling prior knowledge, developing questions

Prepare your aviation unit for takeoff with this informative activity. In advance, enlarge and cut out the jet pattern on page 92. Label the cutout with the word *flight;* then mount it at the top of a sheet of blue bulletin board paper. Below the jet, glue three large cloud cutouts on the paper.

Prior to introducing your aviation unit, ask students to name things they already *know* about flight. List their comments on the first cloud; label it "K." Next, ask them what they *want* to know about flight, and list their suggestions on the second cloud with the heading "W." Delay your final question until after you have completed your aviation unit. At that time, ask students to name things they *learned* about flight during their studies. List students' thoughts on the remaining cloud labeled with "L." Then review your unit by reading the completed display.

Life Before Flight 🖥

Identifying ways advances in transportation changed lives

It's hard to imagine that less than 100 years ago there were no flying machines! Today the sky's the limit when it comes to aviation exploration, and National Aviation Day (August 19) is the perfect time to honor the science and art of flying. The date also honors the birthday of Orville Wright, whose early experiments—with the help of his brother, Wilbur—intrigued the world with flying machines.

To commemorate this day, discuss the many modes of flight that are now available; then ask your youngsters to imagine the days before machines could fly and discuss the differences. Give a copy of "Fabulous Flight" (on page 92) to each child. Ask each student to write his name and a description of one way our lives have changed because of the ability to fly. Enlarge, color, and cut out the biplane pattern on page 92; then mount it on a classroom wall. Arrange students' writings on a banner trailing the plane as shown.

Flight

K
• ...nes fly in the sky.
• P...nes have wings.
• Pilots fly planes.
• Planes take off on a runway.

W
• How does a plane fly?
• How does a hot-air balloon work?

L

Flight Experience 🖥

Making a personal connection, responding to a writing prompt

Use this picture graph to chart your students' flight experience. To prepare the graph, cover a bulletin board with blue paper and title the board "Our Flight Experience." Create a runway from bulletin board paper or construction paper and staple it to the bottom of the display; then add cotton or paper clouds. Next, have each student color, cut out, and personalize a copy of the jet pattern on page 92. To gather information to complete your graph, ask each child about his flight experience. If a student has flown, staple his jet near the clouds. If a child has not flown in an airplane, staple his cutout to the runway. For a follow-up activity, assign a writing topic to the students in each group. For those who have flown, ask them to write about a flying experience. For those who have not, ask them to write about a destination they would like to fly to in the future.

Just the "Plane" Facts!

Identifying plane parts and the purposes they serve

What better way to begin your aviation unit than to introduce students to the numerous types of airplanes! To do this, read aloud *The Airplane Alphabet Book* by Jerry Pallotta and Fred Stillwell. In this unique ABC book, each alphabet letter is accompanied by information specific to airplanes. After sharing the book, give a copy of "The 'Plane' Facts" on page 90 to each student. Discuss the meanings of the words in the word box; then instruct students to complete the sentences using the words and color as indicated. Soon your students will be tossing out terms like *fuselage* as if they've been aviators all their lives!

Up, Up, and Away

Communicating observations, constructing reasonable explanations

This hot-air experiment will remind your students that not all flying machines are airplanes. Experiments were done with hot-air balloons as early as the late 1700s by the Montgolfier brothers from France. They began experimenting by filling paper bags with smoke. At first they thought the smoke made the bags ascend, but they later learned the hot air caused the bags to rise. In September of 1783, they launched a balloon carrying a sheep, a duck, and a rooster. The flight lasted about eight minutes, and the animals landed safely. In November, two humans stayed aloft for 25 minutes. The age of flight had begun!

Prove the effects of different air temperatures inside a balloon with the following demonstration. Tape the open end of a dry-cleaning bag to a paper tube. Also tape the small opening at the top of the bag. Aim a hair dryer (with variable temperature settings) into the bag as shown. Change the settings during the experiment and ask students to observe and comment on what happens to the bag when the temperatures change. Now that's uplifting research!

Airport Array

Reading and interpreting a map

Your students' map-reading skills will soar as they complete this activity. Give each child a copy of "Airport Array" on page 91. Have each child color and cut out the six passengers at the side of the page. Then ask each child to use the information provided to glue the passengers in their correct locations.

1.

2.

3.

4.

Repeat Steps 2, 3, and 4 for other half of plane.

5.

Airplane Engineers
Conducting a simple science investigation

Engage your students in this high-flying aerodynamic experiment. Explain to your class that as any object moves through air it experiences *drag,* or resistance. Engineers who design airplanes try to create sleek designs that will cut through the air with little drag. Ask your students to become airplane engineers. Have each child use duplicating paper to create several paper airplanes—searching for a design that will best avoid drag. Use the basic airplane design shown on this page to get your students started, but encourage them to experiment with original creations. After students have had a chance to experiment with several creations, have each child decorate and personalize his best plane. Then conduct a contest to determine which child's airplane flies the farthest or the fastest. Enlist students' help in investigating the winning airplane for signs of its success.

Futuristic Flight
Producing artwork to communicate an idea

Though not likely to fly, these futuristic flying machines will showcase your students' creativity. Use the recipe shown to create a supply of sculpting dough for your class (or, if desired, use Crayola® Model Magic®). Divide the mixture among your students and ask them to design flying machines of the future. Provide dry pasta, glitter, or sequins for embellishing their designs. Allow the creations to dry for several days; then display the fleet of flyers on a table for everyone to see. What a fun way to focus on the future!

Sculpting Dough

Makes enough for about six students.

Ingredients:
3 c. flour
1 1/2 c. salt
1 c. water

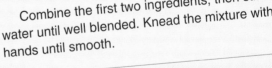

Combine the first two ingredients; then stir in the water until well blended. Knead the mixture with your hands until smooth.

Flight Food
Following directions

These healthful treats are just "plane" fun! To make one treat, have each child spread cream cheese on a celery stick. Then have her place a carrot stick across the celery to create wings. To make the plane's tail, have her place a shorter carrot stick, end first, into the cheese as shown. Have her use a dab of cream cheese to attach a pretzel propeller. Your students will gobble up these tasty treats before they have a chance to take flight!

Lift Off With Literature

Clevell Harris

I ate apples in Argentina.
I played the piano in Peru.
I caught catfish in Canada.
I sang songs in Switzerland.
I bought bananas in Brazil.

Will and Orv 💻
by Walter A. Schulz
Developing a sense of time

Imagine witnessing the first motorized airplane flight made by Wilbur and Orville Wright! This story will help you do just that. In this retelling, the historic 12-second ride is described from the viewpoint of young Johnny Moore—one of five who watched the event.

Help your students relate to the seemingly short 12-second flight time with this activity. Prepare by making a list of activities—some that take more than 12 seconds to complete, and some that take less. Give a copy of the list to each student; then pair your students and give each twosome a stopwatch. Ask one person from each pair to try an activity from the list while his partner times him. If the activity can be completed in 12 seconds or less, have the partners put check marks on their papers next to that activity. What a timely way to teach about the first flight!

Amelia's Fantastic Flight
by Rose Bursik
Using alliteration in writing

Take flight with this imaginative little girl who not only builds and repairs her own airplane, but flies it around the world! This fictional flight is extra fantastic because of its scenic pictures and informative maps. To add interest to the text, the author uses alliteration to introduce each new country that Amelia explores.

Turn your students into explorers like Amelia and acquaint them with alliteration by having them make their own fantastic flight booklets. To make a booklet, stack three 8 1/2" x 11" sheets of white paper and hold the pages vertically in front of you. Slide the top sheet upward approximately one inch; then repeat the process for the second sheet. Next, fold the paper thicknesses forward to create six graduated layers or pages (see the illustration). Staple close to the fold. Then have each child write her title on the top sheet. On each page have the student write a sentence using alliteration to tell about her trip to five countries of her choice. Have students add drawings to complete their adventures.

Hot-Air Henry
by Mary Calhoun
Narrative writing

Introduce students to another fabulous flying phenomenon—the hot-air balloon—with this fictitious story. Students' imaginations will soar with Henry as he hops aboard his owner's hot-air balloon for a beautiful adventure.

Ask your students to imagine looking down on Earth as Henry did. What part of the world would they most want to see? Have each child make a drawing of his image on a 12-inch paper circle. Then have him write about his scene on a six-inch paper square. Add strings to create hot-air balloon shapes as shown and display them around the classroom.

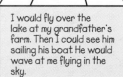

I would fly over the lake at my grandfather's farm. Then I could see him sailing his boat. He would wave at me flying in the sky.

Joey

89

The "Plane" Facts

Complete each sentence.
Use the word box.
Color the plane as directed.

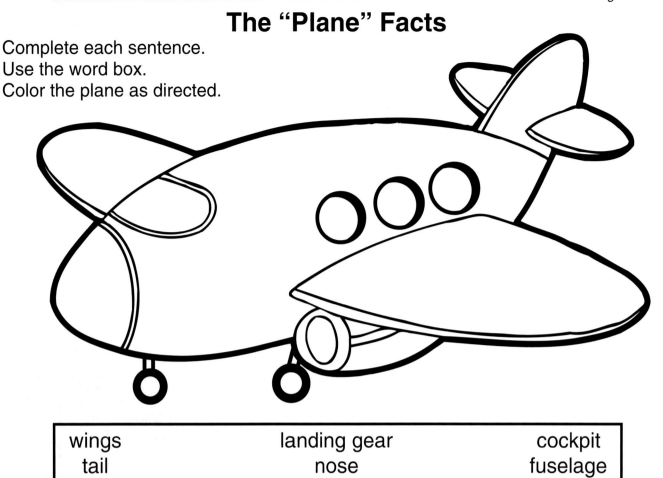

wings	landing gear	cockpit
tail	nose	fuselage

1. The _____ is where you find the pilot. Color it blue.

2. The _____ is the front-most section of the plane. Color it red.

3. The _____ supports the plane when it's on the ground. Color it orange.

4. The _____ helps guide the plane. This section is at the back of the plane. Color it brown.

5. The _____ is the central body of the plane. It is from the nose to the tail. You will find passengers and cargo here. Color it green.

6. The _____ create lift and raise the plane into the air. Color them yellow.

Airport Array

These passengers are at the airport. Can you decide where each person belongs?
Read each statement. Cut and glue to show where each passenger belongs.

1. "I'm driving east on Airline Avenue. I hope I'm not late for my flight!"
2. "My flight leaves soon, so I'm waiting in the southwest corner of the terminal."
3. "I'm getting my rental car from the building directly east of the parking garage."
4. "I'm picking up my luggage from the east wing of the terminal."
5. "My flight is leaving from Runway One right now!"
6. "I had a safe landing. Now I'm getting into my car in the parking garage."

Bonus Box:
Research to find out what the building labeled "Hangar" is used for. Write about it on another sheet of paper.

North

Hangar

East

Airline Avenue

Parking Garage

Airport Drive

Terminal

Runway One

West

South

1.
2.
3.
4.
5.
6.

Note to the teacher: Use with "Airport Array" on page 87.

Biplane Pattern
Use with "Life Before Flight" on page 86.

Jet Pattern
Use with "Time for Takeoff" on page 86
and "Flight Experience" on page 87.

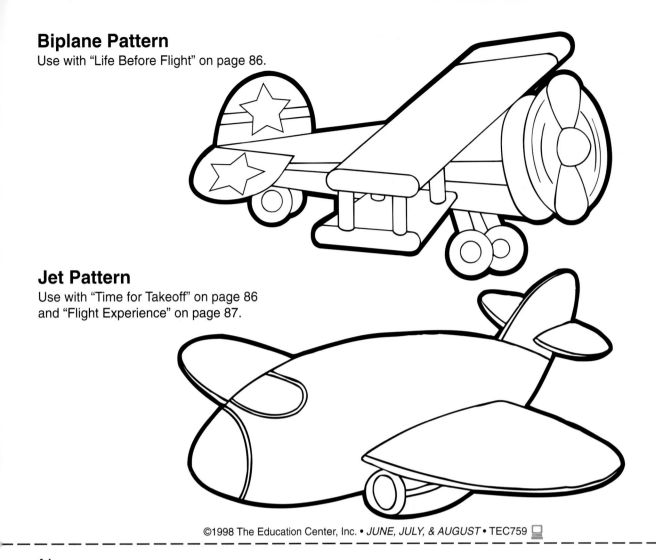

Name _____ *Aviation: writing*

Fabulous Flight

Note to the teacher: Use with "Life Before Flight" on page 86.

Answer Keys

Page 34

```
B  D  E  F  G  E  U  O  T  T  C  B  T  R
C  O  C  K  R  O  A  C  H  K  R  U  P  S
L  W  N  L  A  D  Y  B  U  G  N  T  U  I
M  P  X  U  S  A  E  J  R  V  P  T  H  L
O  L  M  O  S  Q  U  I  T  O  F  E  C  K
U  S  W  S  H  E  W  F  Q  R  K  R  M  W
D  R  A  G  O  N  F  L  Y  N  B  F  C  O
Y  I  E  Z  P  K  U  E  M  G  H  L  F  R
B  E  E  F  P  J  R  A  E  W  F  Y  D  M
M  N  L  R  E  W  Q  F  C  N  M  S  L  Y
P  U  T  E  R  M  I  T  E  U  F  D  E  W
```

Page 90

1. cockpit
2. nose
3. landing gear
4. tail
5. fuselage
6. wings

Page 91

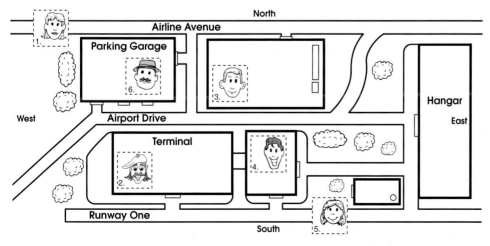

Bonus Box: A hangar is an enclosed area for housing and repairing aircraft.

Index